PROFESSIONAL LIABILITY *and* RISK MANAGEMENT

An Essential Guide for Obstetrician–Gynecologists

Second Edition

The American College of
Obstetricians and Gynecologists
Women's Health Care Physicians

Professional Liability and Risk Management: An Essential Guide for Obstetrician–Gynecologists, Second Edition, was developed by the staff of the Department of Professional Liability/Risk Management of the American College of Obstetricians and Gynecologists.

Department of Professional Liability/Risk Management

Staff:

Albert L. Strunk, JD, MD, FACOG, Deputy Executive Vice President and
Vice President of Fellowship Activities
James Lumalcuri, MSW, Director, Research and Education
Nonda Wilson, MS, Manager, Research and Special Projects
Donna Kovacheva, Executive Assistant

Consultant: Rebecca Kelly

The Department of Professional Liability/Risk Management gratefully acknowledges the contributions of the following individuals:

ACOG's Committee on Professional Liability

Members, 2004:

Larry L. Veltman, MD, FACOG, Chair
Steven Kahner, MD, FACOG, Vice Chair
Joy G. Cavalaris, MD

Paul F. Fairbrother, MD, FACOG
Lisa M. Hollier, MD FACOG
Patricia M. Miller, MD, FACOG

Members, 2007:

Lisa M. Hollier, MD, FACOG, Chair
Stewart J. Wetchler, MD, FACOG, Vice Chair
Stella M. Dantas, MD, FACOG
Philip J. Diamond, MD, FACOG
Jennifer M. Keller, MD
Sindhu Srinivas, MD

National Officers of ACOG's Junior Fellow College Advisory Council

Leah Kaufman, MD, JFCAC, Chair
May Hsieh Blanchard, MD, JFCAC, Vice Chair
Wanjiku N. Kabiru, MD, JFCAC, Past Chair

ACOG's Legal Affairs Department
Susannah Frazier, JD, Staff Attorney

Library of Congress Cataloging-in-Publication Data

Professional liability and risk management : an essential guide for obstetrician/gynecologists/developed by the staff of the Department of Professional Liability/Risk Management of the American College of Obstetricians and Gynecologists. -- 2nd ed.

p. cm

Includes bibliographical references and index.

ISBN 978-1-932328-47-9 (alk. paper)

1. Gynecologists--Malpractice--United States. 2. Obstetricians--Malpractice--United States. 3. Hospitals--Risk management--United States. 4. Risk management--United States. I. American College of Obstetricians and Gynecologists. Women's Health Care Physicians. II. American College of Obstetricians and Gynecologists. Dept. of Professional Liability/Risk Management.

KF2910.G943P769 2008
344.7304'121--dc22

2008003792

Professional Liability and Risk Management: An Essential Guide for Obstetrician–Gynecologists, Second Edition, provides risk management information that is current as of the date issued and is subject to change. This document does not define a standard of care nor should it be interpreted as legal advice. As always, physicians should consult their personal attorneys about legal requirements in their jurisdictions and for legal advice on particular matters. ACOG makes no representations or warranties, expressed or implied, regarding the accuracy of the information contained in this book and disclaims any liability or responsibility for any consequences resulting from or otherwise related to any use of, or reliance on, this book.

Referral to Internet sites does not imply the endorsement of the American College of Obstetricians and Gynecologists. References to such web sites are not meant to be comprehensive; the exclusion of a web site does not reflect the quality of that web site. Please note that web sites and uniform resource locators are subject to change without warning. Many of these pages provide basic information but have links with more detailed information and resources.

Copies of *Professional Liability and Risk Management: An Essential Guide for Obstetrician–Gynecologists*, Second Edition, can be purchased through the ACOG Distribution Center by calling toll free 1-800-762-2264. Orders also can be purchased through the ACOG web site at www.acog.org.

12345/21098

Contents

Preface

The American College of Obstetricians and Gynecologists (ACOG) has long been a leader among medical professional societies in providing educational materials to its members about professional liability and risk management. As early as 1982, ACOG established a Department of Professional Liability and began to teach its members about the unexpected, sometimes obscure and seemingly unfair, elements of civil litigation. Those early materials have stood the test of time, and readers of earlier ACOG liability publications will recognize in this second edition of *Professional Liability and Risk Management: An Essential Guide for Obstetrician–Gynecologists* the reiteration of certain basic principles. Unfortunately, ACOG members, while better informed about the civil litigation process, have nevertheless experienced increasing liability insurance premiums, increasing fear of less-than-optimal patient outcomes, increasing litigation alleging negligent care, and increasing indemnity awards to plaintiffs.

No one, except perhaps a personal injury lawyer, would claim that the current system is fair to either patients or physicians. To the contrary, a number of respected studies show that the current system is wasteful, inequitable, and time-consuming. The only consistent correlation has been between size of indemnity award and severity of injury, whether the medical care was good or bad. Medical liability litigation costs our nation between $60 billion and $120 billion each year, depending on whose analysis one accepts. Less than 40% of these dollars reach injured patients. Physicians, however, often are held liable for very unfortunate and sad patient outcomes that are in no way a result of medical professional negligence.

At the same time, we cannot ignore the reality of medical error. It is true that the overwhelming majority of these errors involve medication errors and non-medical personnel, but the reality of negligence by physicians cannot be denied. The processes of improving patient safety and diminishing the risk of medical error are opposite sides of the same coin. In addition to matters of professional liability, this book teaches management practices that will improve patient safety while diminishing medical–legal risk.

It remains unclear whether federal tort reform will ever be achieved and to what extent reform will be adopted at the state level. Tort reform will, in any event, be only one step toward addressing the legitimate needs of patients, physicians, and our society. A new system of medical justice might achieve the fundamental changes necessary to overhaul a costly, inefficient, and inequitable system of health care and correct a flawed system of determining medical liability. However, there is a small but influential body of opinion that holds that the patient–physician relationship must be recast in contract, rather than tort, if meaningful change is to be achieved. Although ACOG continues to fight for these larger goals, it recognizes that our Fellow and Junior Fellow members must continue to receive relevant and current educational materials to be prepared to face the reality of civil litigation as it exists today.

This work is intended as much for residents in training and physicians newly in practice as it is for those more worldly wise in matters of litigation, risk management, and the management of litigation-related stress. Significant changes have been made from earlier ACOG publications. Information is presented in a "quick-read" format that we hope will facilitate rapid comprehension, even amidst the stress of litigation. We have tried to weave important risk-management concepts into the fabric of the overall liability message. Throughout the text, a number of issues that especially affect residents have been expanded, and we have devoted a separate chapter to unique resident concerns. We also have expanded our discussion of the legal basis for claims other than tort, especially claims arising out of statutory requirements. Finally, we have included chapters on emerging legal issues and expert witness testimony. In all of this, the text is supplemented with a medical–legal glossary, several appendixes containing many useful references, and an index.

We hope you will find this second edition of *Professional Liability and Risk Management: An Essential Guide for Obstetrician–Gynecologists* a useful, if not indispensable, resource with which to educate yourself about the fundamentals of professional liability litigation and risk management. Data suggest that you will sooner or later be ensnared by the growth industry of civil litigation. Now is the time to prepare yourself. We hope you will find this publication to be a useful tool both to reduce medical error and to defend against false allegations of medical negligence. If it is of such use, it also will have made a small contribution to a larger cause, ensuring continued access to quality health care for the women of America.

Albert L. Strunk, JD, MD, FACOG
Deputy Executive Vice President and Vice President of Fellowship Activities
The American College of Obstetricians and Gynecologists

Professional Liability *and* Risk Management

An Essential Guide for Obstetrician–Gynecologists

Second Edition

Chapter 1

Elements of Professional Liability

Professional Liability and Risk Management: An Essential Guide for Obstetrician–Gynecologists begins with an introduction to the fundamental legal principles of medical professional liability. You became an ob-gyn to care for patients, not to practice law, but medical liability issues will be with you every day from residency training through retirement. Gaining an understanding of the legal concepts and vocabulary of professional liability cannot guarantee that you will never be sued. However, knowing the legal basis of medical liability may help you reduce your chances of a lawsuit. If you are sued, a working knowledge of the legal issues that underlie medical liability claims will better prepare you to defend yourself and cope with the effects of a lawsuit. This chapter addresses the following legal issues:

- Negligence and medical professional liability

- Duty of care

- Breach of duty

- Causation

- Damages

Negligence and Medical Professional Liability

Every individual has a common law duty to take reasonable steps to avoid injuring other people. As a driver, for example, you are obligated to exercise "due care" so that other people are not hurt. If you do not drive with the degree of care that a reasonable, ordinarily cautious driver would use under similar circumstances and you injure someone, you are negligent. Simply put, medical professional liability is negligence in carrying out medical duties.

A medical liability lawsuit is a civil action filed by a patient against a physician that asks for monetary compensation for physical, mental, or financial injury caused by the physician's professional negligence. The person initiating the action (eg, the patient) is the plaintiff. The person against whom the action is filed (the physician) is the defendant. These terms differ somewhat from those used in a criminal trial. The party initiating a criminal action (the state or federal government) is the prosecution and the person accused of the crime is the defendant.

If the jury finds that there is a 51% likelihood that the plaintiff's allegations are true, you will lose the case.

If a patient sues you for professional liability, she must prove the following:

- You owed her a duty of care.
- You breached that duty.
- Your breach of duty (your negligence) caused her injury.
- She suffered damages as a result of that injury.

The patient/plaintiff must prove all four of these elements by what is known as a "preponderance of the evidence." This means only that it is more likely than not that you had a duty to her, breached that duty, and caused her injury, and she suffered damages. In other words, if the jury finds that there is a 51% likelihood that the plaintiff's allegations are true, you will lose the case. This is not the same standard of proof you use in making clinical decisions and interpreting scientific data. It also differs from the standard of proof required in criminal proceedings. In a criminal trial, the defendant must be proved guilty "beyond a reasonable doubt." The criminal standard of proof is analogous to a greater than 99% chance that the defendant is guilty.

Duty of Care

As a physician, you have a duty of care to your patient that begins when you establish a physician–patient relationship with her—that is, when you offer to treat her and she accepts your services. You are free to choose not to establish a relationship with an individual patient, with a few exceptions:

- If you are a resident, you typically cannot choose your patients.
- Residents or attending physicians cannot refuse to treat an emergency room patient.
- Federal law restricts your ability to transfer or refuse to treat patients with emergency medical conditions, including women in active labor. (See Chapter 12, "Government Requirements Affecting Medical Practice," for information on the Emergency Medical Treatment and Labor Act.)

Although contact with a patient usually is necessary to establish a physician–patient relationship and your duty of care, there are circumstances in which such relationships may be established without face-to-face contact with the patient. For example, providing advice over the telephone or through e-mail can mark the establishment of the physician–patient relationship. In some circumstances—if the patient is a member of a managed care plan or among members of a capitated patient list, or if the appointment is for treatment of a life-threatening condition—the physician–patient relationship might begin when a patient makes her appointment.

Breach of Duty

Although the patient who sues you must prove that you owed her a duty of care, most medical professional liability cases focus on the question of whether you breached that duty. The patient must prove either:

- An "act of commission": you did something you should not have done, or

- An "act of omission": you failed to do something you should have done.

To decide whether you breached your duty to the patient, the court must first define that duty. In general, a physician's duty is to provide treatment that is consistent with the standard of care. The phrase "standard of care" might suggest that there is a single, well known, and unambiguous yardstick that determines whether you provided appropriate care. Your experience as a physician probably has taught you that such unambiguous yardsticks for medical practice do not exist.

What does standard of care mean, then, for legal purposes? The law defines standard of care as care that would ordinarily be provided by physicians practicing in the same specialty. Do not think that you have missed the point if you find this explanation somewhat lacking in clarity! In real world practice, courts define the standard of care within the context of an individual patient's clinical circumstances.

If a patient files a medical liability claim against you, how will a court define the standard of care? Most often, testimony from an expert witness establishes the standard of care the court will apply. A case decided by the New Jersey Superior Court, *Morlino v. Medical Center of Ocean County*, 295 N.J. Super. 113 (App. Div. 1996), offers an example of the need for expert testimony to establish the standard of care:

- A pregnant woman visited an emergency room for treatment of a sore throat. The emergency room physician prescribed an antibiotic. The fetus later died.

- The patient sued, alleging that the antibiotic had caused an allergic reaction that killed her fetus.

- The patient proffered as evidence of negligence a *Physician's Desk Reference* (PDR) warning against using the drug for pregnant women because the risk of harm to the fetus could not be ruled out.

- The jury decided in favor of the defendants. The patient appealed.

- The Superior Court upheld the jury's decision, stating that the PDR warning alone, without expert testimony, was not adequate to establish the standard of care.

Chapter 3, "Scientific Evidence and the Role of the Expert Witness," provides more detailed discussion of expert witness testimony.

There are some circumstances in which the plaintiff does not need expert witness testimony to establish the standard of care. Under the doctrine of *res ipsa loquitur,* the event itself demonstrates negligence. For example, if the case involves a surgical clamp discovered in the patient's abdomen after surgery, the very fact that the clamp was left behind is proof of negligence; a physician providing appropriate care would not accidentally leave a surgical instrument in the patient's abdomen. The effect of *res ipsa loquitur* varies from state to state:

- In some states, the burden of proof shifts to the defendant.

- In other states, it imposes a burden on the defendant to go forward with countervailing evidence against the charge of negligence. For example, the physician would need to produce evidence that, under the specific circumstances, the act was not negligent.

Expert witness testimony is also not needed if there is evidence establishing a standard of care that meets a common knowledge test. A classic example is a case decided by the New Jersey Supreme Court in 1961, *Sanzari v. Rosenfeld,* 34 N.J. 128 (1961):

- A patient with severe hypertension died after a dentist gave him an anesthetic containing epinephrine.

- The plaintiff used the manufacturer's package insert as evidence that administering epinephrine to a patient with hypertension violated the standard of care.

- The court determined that the package insert provided the jury with enough evidence to use its common knowledge in determining the standard of care.

The court determines whether the jury can make a decision based on common knowledge. The evidence presented must be of a type that ordinary jurors can understand using their fund of common knowledge. For example, written evidence would need to be in plain language and not filled with technical terms usually understood only by professionals in the field. The evidence also would need to provide enough information for the jury to make a decision.

In some instances, a court might recognize national medical specialty guidelines (for example, ACOG Practice Bulletins or American Cancer Society recommendations) or a hospital protocol as the relevant standard of care. Adhering to national guidelines and hospital policies offers some protection in a medical liability case. Many medical guidelines and protocols are open to some degree of interpretation, so following them is not a guarantee of protection. Failing to follow relevant national medical guidelines or hospital protocols makes a medical liability claim more difficult to defend.

If you are a resident, you should realize that a court most likely would apply the same standard of care to you as to a fully trained, board-certified ob-gyn. (See Chapter 9, "Special Liability Issues for Residents," for more discussion of this issue.)

Causation

In addition to proving it is more likely than not that you owed a duty of care and breached that duty—that is, you provided treatment that did not meet the standard of care—the patient must prove that your negligence directly caused her injury. Causation is the most difficult element of the medical professional liability claim to prove. Patients usually rely on expert witness testimony to prove causation. Evidence of causation must prove that your negligence caused the injury to a "reasonable degree of medical probability." The patient does not need to demonstrate absolute proof or proof beyond a reasonable doubt.

Damages

If a patient proves that she suffered physical, financial, or emotional injury as a result of your negligence, the jury or court can award her damages (monetary compensation for her injuries). The following categories of damages are the most common:

- Special damages
- General damages
- Punitive or exemplary damages

Special Damages

Special damages—also called economic damages—compensate the patient for expenses that can be proved to be directly caused by the injury:

- Medical expenses
- Rehabilitation costs
- Lost wages

General Damages

Patients may receive general damages—also known as noneconomic damages—as compensation for the intangible natural consequences of the injury:

- Pain and suffering (both physical and emotional or mental)
- Disfigurement
- Interference with ordinary enjoyment of life
- Loss of consortium (the patient's parent, spouse, or child may make a claim for damages for the loss of care, comfort, and society and, if applicable, interference with sexual relations)

Punitive or Exemplary Damages

The court may award punitive damages in addition to compensation for actual expenses and intangible damages. Plaintiffs in medical professional liability cases often ask for but rarely receive punitive damages. Punitive damages seek to punish egregious or outrageous conduct, even if not intentional. Coverage for punitive damages is, in most cases, excluded by policies of medical professional liability insurance. Punitive damages might be awarded if a physician:

- Showed reckless disregard for a patient's well-being
- Provided clearly incompetent treatment
- Provided care while under the influence of alcohol or drugs
- Failed to respond to multiple calls to go to the hospital
- Engaged in criminal behavior

Understanding the core principles of medical liability introduced in this chapter is important for any ob-gyn. The next chapter will continue the discussion by presenting several emerging legal theories that can change how the basic model of medical liability might be applied. For a more detailed discussion of a physician defendant's role in the civil litigation process, see Appendix A, "What To Do If You Are Sued."

KEY POINTS

✓ Medical professional liability is negligence in carrying out medical duties.

✓ The patient must prove duty, breach of duty, causation, and damages.

✓ The standard of proof for medical negligence is a preponderance of the evidence—more likely than not.

✓ Expert witnesses usually are needed to provide evidence of the standard of care and causation.

Chapter 2

Emerging Legal Theories

In Chapter 1 you learned about the basic elements and legal doctrines underlying medical professional liability. It is important to realize that, in practice, there are some significant departures from the fairly simple, straightforward model outlined in Chapter 1. In large measure, these differences reflect a broad trend in our society toward expanding access to the courts for people who believe they have been injured, making it easier for plaintiffs to prove alleged negligence and causation, and providing little guidance to lay jurors in assessing damages. Equally significant are increasing public demands that medical professionals and businesses be held accountable for actions that may have harmed someone.

This chapter will introduce several emerging legal theories that can affect physician defendants in medical liability cases:

- Expansions in scope of duty

- Loss of chance

- Combining and concurring negligence

- Apportioning liability

Expansions in Scope of Duty

In the simple model of medical professional liability outlined in the previous chapter, you owe a duty of care to patients with whom you have established a physician–patient relationship. Proving that you owed a duty of care is the first element in a medical liability case. If you owed no duty of care, there is no case. Courts have increased the responsibilities of potential defendants in medical liability cases by extending the duty of care beyond the patient herself. You could be found to have a duty of care to everyone who might reasonably be affected by the care you provide to the patient. For example, if a patient dies due to your alleged negligence, her spouse and children might be able to sue you for emotional distress on their own behalf, as well as for damages on behalf of the patient's estate.

The nature of the care you provide as an ob-gyn makes the issue of expanded scope of duty particularly significant. Many of the diagnostic and treatment services that ob-gyns provide are closely tied to fertility, childbearing, and other

Courts have increased the responsibilities of potential defendants in medical liability cases by extending the duty of care beyond the patient herself.

family issues. An adverse outcome in ob-gyn care can affect not just the patient, but her spouse, her fetus if she is pregnant, and any future pregnancies as well:

- You may diagnose a condition that could affect the outcome of a patient's future pregnancies.
- Future children might be injured as a result of the condition. If you failed to notify the patient and her spouse of the risk, the patient might have a cause of action against you.

In some circumstances, physicians might have a "duty to warn" people other than the patient if there is a risk of harm to those individuals. The duty to warn may conflict with your legal and ethical obligations to protect your patient's privacy and can increase your liability risk in two ways:

1. If you do not warn an individual at risk, and if he or she does suffer harm, you could be sued.
2. If you do disclose information without the patient's permission, she might sue you for violating her privacy.

The best known example of a physician's duty to warn may be that of the psychiatrist who learns that his or her patient is likely to harm another person and is then obligated to inform that person. The duty to warn is not limited to situations in which you know that your patient intends to harm someone. For instance, genetic tests that identify increased risk for specific diseases that develop in adulthood can raise questions of whether you have a duty to warn. A patient may ask to be tested for the inherited *BRCA2* mutation, which increases the risk of breast and ovarian cancer. If her test result is positive, her relatives also may have inherited the same genetic trait and the same increased risk.

Relevant case law is limited, but some courts have found that physicians have a duty to warn affected relatives about positive results of genetic tests. Interpretations of what you must do to fulfill your duty have varied. The American Medical Association's Council on Ethical and Judicial Affairs has developed recommendations for physicians:

- Before your patient has a genetic screening test, discuss the possible need for her to inform at-risk relatives if the result is positive.
- Document the discussion in the medical record.
- Be available to assist your patient in communicating with at-risk relatives if needed.

When you diagnose and treat a patient with an infectious disease, you might also have a duty to warn others who could contract the disease:

- Make sure you are familiar with state laws and regulations that dictate when you must notify authorities (eg, the state health department) that you have diagnosed a particular communicable disease.
- For infectious diseases you are not required to report to authorities, be familiar with state and federal requirements that outline circumstances in which you may (or must) breach the patient's confidentiality to warn those who are at risk if the patient will not give consent.

Loss of Chance

For a patient to sue you for medical professional liability, she must have suffered an injury. The "loss of chance" theory allows a patient to argue that your negligence (eg, you did not promptly diagnose or properly treat her condition) cost her a significant chance for a better outcome, rather than that you caused a specific injury. Accordingly, she may argue that her chance for survival or recovery was eliminated or reduced (*Evers v. Dollinger,* 95 N.J. 399 [1984]).

Under the usual standards for proving that your negligence caused her injury, the patient must prove that, if you had not been negligent, it is more likely than not that she would have survived or recovered. That is, her chances of survival or recovery were 51% or greater. If the likelihood of survival or recovery was 50% or less, the patient cannot win the case. The lost chance doctrine expands the instances in which physicians can be sued when treatment is unsuccessful. The chance of survival or recovery does not have to be 51% or greater. Court decisions in some states suggest that this type of claim might be allowed even if the chance of survival or recovery was significantly less than 50%.

The loss of chance theory reflects a view that physicians should be held accountable for a patient's loss of a chance for survival or recovery even if that chance was relatively small to begin with.

States vary widely in their adoption and interpretation of the lost chance theory. Some states do not recognize this theory at all. Among those that have used the lost chance theory, applications fall into three broad categories:

1. Relaxed causation standard

2. Increased risk of harm

3. Separate injury or cause of action

The lost chance doctrine expands the instances in which physicians can be sued when treatment is unsuccessful.

Relaxed Causation Standard

If courts in your state have established a relaxed causation standard for loss of chance claims, a patient would need only to prove that your failure to follow the standard of care resulted in a significant loss of her chance to recover. For example:

- You did not follow national guidelines for breast cancer screening and thus the patient's breast cancer was diagnosed when she had a 15% chance of survival instead of the 40% chance she would have had if you had followed the screening guidelines.

- She does not have to prove that her treatment would have been successful if you had followed the national guideline, just that she would have had a better chance.

Note that the patient must still prove that you were negligent. If the jury or judge decides that you complied with the accepted guideline or that the guideline did not define the standard of care, you will not be held liable for the loss of chance.

Increased Risk of Harm

Instead of focusing on the loss of or reduction in the chance for survival or recovery, the "increased risk of harm" doctrine deals with situations in which a patient alleges that a physician's negligent treatment put her at increased risk of future harm (*Boryla v. Pash,* 937 P.2d 813 [Colo. App. 1996]). In this case, the plaintiff must prove that:

- The physician's negligence increased her risk of harm

- The increased risk was a substantial factor in causing her injury

Separate Injury or Cause of Action

Some states have defined the loss of chance to achieve the better outcome as the injury to be compensated. The patient has a separate cause of action, meaning that she can file a claim for the loss of chance alone. If the plaintiff proves that it is more likely than not that your negligence reduced her chance of survival or a better outcome, she can be awarded damages. She does not have to prove that your negligence was more likely than not the cause of her ultimate injury.

Under this approach, damages are based on the value of the lost chance. For example, if your actions resulted in a 30% reduction in the chance that the patient would survive, damages could be only 30% of damages awarded if your actions were 100% responsible for the patient's death. If you are involved in a case in which loss of chance or increased risk of harm is alleged, be prepared:

- Be sure your defense team is familiar with courts' interpretation of these doctrines in your state.

- Have an expert witness who can provide effective testimony about statistical issues related to the patient's condition.

Combining and Concurring Negligence

Many other health care providers can be involved in your patient's care, especially if she has a complex condition. Under the doctrine of combining and concurring negligence, you could be held liable for damages even if negligent care provided by another provider was a more important factor in causing the patient's injury than errors you made. Consider the following example:

- A physician negligently failed to control bleeding during surgery.

- The patient required a blood transfusion.

- The patient suffered a transfusion reaction due to the blood bank's failure to properly type and match the patient's blood.

- The physician's negligence in failing to control the patient's bleeding combined and concurred with the blood bank's negligence.

Apportioning Liability

If you are involved in a medical professional liability case that names multiple defendants, your share of the damages will depend on whether your state follows one of the followng doctrines:

- Joint and several liability
- Proportional liability

Joint and Several Liability

Joint and several liability is known as the "deep pocket" rule. Under joint and several liability:

- Each defendant is responsible for the full amount of damages awarded in the lawsuit, regardless of his or her relative responsibility for the injury.

- You could bear the least amount of responsibility for the patient's injury but be required to pay all damages if other defendants in the case are uninsured and have no assets that can be seized to pay the damages.

Proportional Liability

In contrast to joint and several liability, the theory of proportional liability allocates responsibility for damages based on each defendant's relative amount of blame for the injury:

- If the court is able to allocate accurately the share of blame to each defendant, the theory of proportional liability can be applied.

- If a jury found that your errors contributed only 25% to a patient's injury, and the other provider's negligence contributed 75%, you would pay only 25% of the damages awarded.

Proportional liability seems to be more equitable and its enactment has been a goal of tort reform efforts. State laws vary, though, with some directing the burden of large awards away from the physician if there are other defendants (eg, hospital, pharmaceutical manufacturer). The relative advantages of proportional liability and joint and several liability may depend on whether or not you are the "deep pocket." The best practical advice is to know your state law and protect your assets accordingly. (See Chapter 10, "Professional Liability Insurance," for a discussion of medical professional liability insurance and asset protection.)

KEY POINTS

✓ Your duty of care may extend beyond the patient you treat.

✓ Be aware of your potential duty to warn when ordering genetic tests and diagnosing and treating communicable diseases.

✓ The loss of chance doctrine allows a patient to recover damages for a reduced chance of survival or a better outcome.

✓ If you are subject to joint and several liability, you could be responsible for all damages in a case if other defendants cannot or do not pay.

✓ Proportional liability allocates damages based on an individual defendant's share of the blame for injury.

Chapter 3

Scientific Evidence and the Role of the Expert Witness

A medical professional liability claim nearly always involves clinical and scientific issues that typical members of a jury are not qualified to evaluate. Because of this, expert witnesses take part in almost all medical liability trials. Expert witness testimony helps the court determine:

- The relevant standard of care

- Whether the physician met that standard

- Whether a failure to meet the standard of care caused the plaintiff's injury

If you are sued for medical liability, both you and the plaintiff probably will call on expert witnesses to provide evidence. Alternatively, you may serve as an expert witness for either the defendant or plaintiff in a medical liability case. You should understand what the expert witness contributes to the litigation process and what is expected of the expert witness. This chapter discusses:

- Role of expert witness testimony

- Expert witness qualifications

- Expert witness conduct and responsibilities

- The advisability of serving as your own expert

Role of Expert Witness Testimony

As you learned in Chapter 1, the plaintiff in a medical professional liability case must prove four elements to win the case:

1. Duty of care

2. Breach of duty

3. Causation

4. Damages

Either party to the case may use expert witness testimony to address any of the four elements. Most often, though, expert witnesses focus on the standard of care (breach of duty) and causation.

Some witnesses in a medical liability case are "fact witnesses." They testify only about the chain of events leading up to and following the incident that led to the lawsuit—what happened and when. In contrast, the role of the expert witness is not to establish the facts, but to interpret them. The expert witness explains the scientific evidence to a lay jury so that jurors can decide:

- What the evidence means

- Whether the evidence supports the plaintiff or the defendant

- How much weight to give the evidence

An effective expert witness will help the jury and the judge understand the clinical issues involved in the case and will provide an opinion to be considered by the jury in its assessment of the care in question. Additional evidence (textbooks or national guidelines, for example) also can support and reinforce the opinion. Even more important, the opinion must be relevant to the facts in the case.

Expert Witness Qualifications

The court trying the medical professional liability case must qualify an individual to testify as an expert witness. A judge will determine whether someone is qualified to testify. A losing plaintiff or defendant may raise questions about qualification or disqualification of an expert witness during an appeal, if appropriate objections are made during the trial.

The crucial question is whether the individual knows enough about the relevant standards of care and the clinical issues in the case to offer an expert opinion. In some circumstances, an expert witness could be a nonphysician or a physician outside the specialty of the physician being sued if he or she demonstrates expertise that convinces the judge of his or her base of knowledge.

The federal court system has uniform guidelines for qualifying expert witnesses and admitting scientific evidence. For the most part, state courts have not adopted those guidelines. Unfortunately, most medical professional liability cases are heard in state courts that often have the following characteristics:

- Judges seem to prefer to "let the jury decide."

- State judges tend to be relatively lenient in qualifying expert witnesses.

- Judges usually will instruct the jury to consider the expert witness's credentials in deciding how much weight to give his or her testimony.

The American College of Obstetricians and Gynecologists (ACOG) has developed criteria for physician expert witnesses (see Appendix B, "Qualifications for the Physician Expert Witness"). The College believes a physician expert witness should have the following qualifications:

- A current and unrestricted medical license

- Current certification by a specialty board recognized by the American Board of Medical Specialties

- Demonstrated competence in the subject of the case

- Specialty training and clinical experience appropriate to the subject matter in the case

- Knowledge of the standard of care that applied at the time of the alleged incident

- Active involvement in the clinical practice of the specialty or the subject matter of the case within 5 years of the time he or she was asked to be an expert witness

- Past participation in continuing medical education relevant to the case

The College also believes that an expert witness should be prepared to tell the court:

- The percentage of professional time he or she spends testifying in professional liability cases

- The amount of fees and compensation he or she receives for testimony

- The number of times he or she has testified in medical professional liability cases for defendant or plaintiff

The trial can result in a fair and appropriate outcome only if the expert witnesses in the case provide accurate, fair testimony.

If you are sued, make sure your attorney is familiar with ACOG's criteria. Although it is unlikely that the judge hearing your case will use the ACOG criteria to qualify expert witnesses, your attorney can question the plaintiff's expert witness about those issues. Making sure that full information about the credentials and experience of the plaintiff's expert is in the record will help the jury give appropriate weight to the expert's testimony. You also should ensure that any expert witnesses who testify on your behalf meet the ACOG criteria.

Expert Witness Conduct and Responsibilities

The integrity of the court system depends on the integrity of the witnesses who testify. Most medical professional liability cases center on issues related to the standard of care and causation—the issues that only expert witnesses may be able to address authoritatively. The trial can result in a fair and appropriate outcome only if the expert witnesses in the case provide accurate, fair testimony.

All Fellows of ACOG should be familiar with the ACOG documents relevant to the conduct of expert witnesses. These include:

- "Expert Witness Affirmation" (see Appendix C)

- "Code of Professional Ethics of the American College of Obstetricians and Gynecologists" (see Appendix D)

- "Expert Testimony." ACOG Committee Opinion No. 374. American College of Obstetricians and Gynecologists. Obstet Gynecol 2007;110: 445–6.

Fellows of the American College of Obstetricians and Gynecologists who serve as expert witnesses for either the plaintiff or defendant are expected to adhere to the professional principles outlined in ACOG's "Expert Witness Affirmation." In brief, ACOG expects Fellows testifying as expert witnesses to:

- Tell the truth

- Evaluate all facts and medical care thoroughly, fairly, and impartially

- Include all relevant information

- Limit evidence and testimony to subjects about which he or she has knowledge and relevant experience

- Refrain from criticizing or condemning care that meets generally accepted standards in use at the time of the incident

- Refuse to endorse practice that does not meet generally accepted standards

- Ensure that testimony is complete, objective, and scientifically based

- Strive to provide evidence that will help the court achieve a fair outcome

- Distinguish between an adverse outcome and substandard care

- Make an effort to determine whether alleged substandard care caused the adverse outcome

- Submit testimony for peer review, if asked

- Refuse to accept compensation that depends on the outcome of the case

If you are currently involved in litigation or if you are sued in the future, be sure your attorney knows about ACOG's "Expert Witness Affirmation." If an expert witness testifies on your behalf, he or she should sign the affirmation. Your attorney can use the affirmation to bolster the expert's qualifications and credibility. If the plaintiff's expert witness has not signed the "Expert Witness Affirmation," your attorney can raise this in cross-examination. If the plaintiff's expert witness has signed the affirmation, your attorney can, nevertheless, cross-examine on the expert's failure to adhere to the requirements of the affirmation.

The Advisability of Serving as Your Own Expert

After reviewing the ACOG criteria for expert witness qualifications, you might come to the conclusion that you would be qualified to serve as your own expert witness if you were sued. Being your own expert witness is probably not the best strategy, though, for several reasons:

- An outside, objective expert witness probably will carry more weight with the jury.

- As a fact witness, you would testify only about the relevant facts in the case.

- If you are a fact witness, you can be asked only questions about what you recall. You do not have to respond to hypothetical questions, which might involve subject matter or alleged facts about which you are not prepared to respond.

The ideal situation is for the physician defendant to be able to testify solely as a fact witness and not an expert witness. The distinction, however, is sometimes blurred:

- The judge might allow the plaintiff's attorney to treat you like an expert witness, asking you to respond to hypothetical questions and render an opinion.

- If you cannot find an independent expert to testify on your behalf, you will have to serve as your own expert.

Objective and accurate expert witness testimony is essential to an equitable outcome in most medical professional liability cases. If you are sued for medical liability, a fair result may depend on the qualifications and ethical behavior of the expert witnesses. If you ever testify as an expert witness, whether for the patient plaintiff or the physician defendant, you have an ethical obligation to meet the requirements outlined in ACOG's "Code of Professional Ethics," "Qualifications for the Physician Expert Witness," and "Expert Witness Affirmation."

KEY POINTS

✓ Fact witnesses testify about the basic facts of the case—what happened, when, where, and how.

✓ Expert witnesses interpret the scientific and clinical evidence and provide opinions about the appropriateness of care, which the jury considers in making its decision.

✓ Physician defendants are usually better off as fact witnesses, not expert witnesses, but sometimes courts blur the distinction.

✓ The decision about whether someone may testify as an expert witness is up to the court.

✓ Criteria for expert witness qualifications and standards for expert witness conduct have been developed by ACOG.

Chapter 4

Informed Consent

Before you perform any procedure or initiate any treatment, your patient must understand the risks and benefits of treatment, as well as alternatives to treatment. She must consent to the treatment. The process of providing this information, answering questions, and obtaining and documenting the patient's consent is known as "informed consent." What did or did not happen during the informed consent process is often an issue in a medical professional liability claim:

- A patient may allege that you did not obtain valid informed consent.
- The claim could assert that you did not fully inform the patient of potential risks.

Obtaining valid informed consent is both an ethical obligation and a legal duty. Careful attention to the informed consent process may help to prevent a lawsuit or strengthen your defense if you are sued.

This chapter will help you gain an understanding of why you must obtain informed consent and how to go about it. The following topics are covered:

- Your obligation to obtain informed consent
- State informed consent laws
- Amount and type of information you must provide
- Obtaining informed consent
- Informed refusal
- Special informed consent rules
- Documenting informed consent

Your Obligation to Obtain Informed Consent

Every individual has the legal right to decide whether to receive medical treatment. This right is based on the principle that an individual must give permission for any intentional "touching" of his or her person. In the absence of that permission, any "touching," including appropriate and necessary medical care, could be considered a battery. If you provide medical care without the patient's explicit or implied permission, you could be liable for violating her rights.

Obtaining valid informed consent is both an ethical obligation and a legal duty.

The law requires a different type of permission for medical care than it does for other types of contact—for example, a haircut. You have a duty to obtain the patient's informed consent for medical care. That is, her consent is valid only if she fully understands the treatment she is being offered, the risks and benefits of treatment, and the alternatives to treatment. Having the patient sign a printed consent form does not satisfy this obligation. You have an affirmative duty to make sure the patient's consent is truly informed. This means you must take active steps to make sure you have fulfilled your obligations under the law. You cannot assume that just because your patient signed the consent form, her consent is valid. She must understand what it is she has agreed to.

You probably feel that a patient should bear some responsibility for gaining an understanding of the medical treatment you recommend by listening to your explanations, carefully reading the consent form, and asking questions if she does not understand. The law, however, places the burden squarely on you. A case decided by the Intermediate Court of Appeals of Hawaii, *Keomaka v. Zakaib*, 811 P.2d 478 (Hawaii App. 1991), emphasizes this point:

- A physician defendant argued that because the patient had signed the consent form without reading it, he or she was partially responsible and should not be able to collect damages.

- The court rejected the physician's argument, deciding that the patient had no affirmative obligation to try to obtain information about the treatment.

- The court stated that a physician cannot fulfill his or her obligation to obtain informed consent by having the patient sign a preprinted form.

State Informed Consent Laws

State statutes and case law govern the informed consent process for medical care. It varies from state to state:

- State statutes may set standards for the amount of information you must provide, or they may dictate the content of informed consent forms.

- Some state laws are broad and apply to many procedures and patients.

- Other state laws focus narrowly on a few procedures or specific groups of patients (eg, sterilization procedures, individuals with mental illnesses).

You should become familiar with and comply with the informed consent laws in your state. This book does not provide a comprehensive listing of state laws affecting the informed consent process. Your state medical society may be able to provide that information.

Amount and Type of Information You Must Provide

You know your patient must be "informed" for her consent to be valid, but how much information is enough? Must you disclose every possible risk, no matter how rare? State law, both statute and case law, determines how much you must tell the patient. *Disclosure standards* (the criteria for deciding what information must be shared with the patient) fall into two major categories:

1. "Reasonable physician" standards
2. "Patient viewpoint" standards

Reasonable Physician Standards

Until fairly recently, determining how much information a physician had to provide for consent to be valid was based on the reasonable physician standard in most informed consent statutes and case law. A physician must inform a patient about the risks and benefits of treatment that a similar physician in the same or a similar community would disclose. In other words, physicians decide what patients need to know.

In some states this type of standard remains in effect. For example, in *Sherwood v. Carter*, 805 P.2d 452 (Idaho 1991), the Supreme Court of Idaho found that the Idaho informed consent law specifically required that a reasonable physician standard determine the amount of information a physician must disclose:

- The case involved a question of whether a physician had provided enough information about risks to a patient having a lymph node biopsy.

- The patient appealed the verdict because the judge had instructed the jury that the physician was obligated to disclose only what another physician in the community would have disclosed.

- The Idaho Supreme Court did not agree with the patient, deciding that the state's informed consent law clearly set a "medical community" standard for disclosure.

Patient Viewpoint Standards

Many, if not most, jurisdictions have moved toward expanding patients' rights to learn about risks and benefits of medical care before giving consent for treatment. A patient viewpoint disclosure standard requires the following:

- You must tell the patient about all risks and benefits that a reasonable person in the situation would want to know to make an informed decision.

- You must disclose any information that might affect a reasonable person's decision about whether to agree to the recommended treatment.

- The amount and type of information you discuss with a patient must be based on what a reasonable patient would want to know.

- You cannot limit the discussion to what you or other community physicians believe is important to discuss or have customarily discussed with the patient.

- The amount of information you are required to disclose is typically greater than it would be if a reasonable physician standard applied.

A subjective patient disclosure standard requires you to know your patient well and understand what will be important in helping her make the decision that is right for her.

Some courts have extended the reasonable patient standard to a more expansive, subjective patient viewpoint standard. Under this type of standard, you must discuss risks and benefits based on what the individual patient would want to know. This type of standard acknowledges that individuals perceive risks and value outcomes differently. For example, a very small risk of injury to a hand might be of little importance in many patients' decision making, but could be a major factor for a patient who is a concert pianist. A subjective patient disclosure standard requires you to know your patient well and understand what will be important in helping her make the decision that is right for her.

A Supreme Court of New Jersey decision, *Largey v. Rothman,* 540 A.2d 504 (N.J. 1988), provides some insight into the thinking behind the trend toward a patient viewpoint disclosure standard:

- A patient claimed that she developed lymphedema from a lymph node biopsy, that she had not been informed this was a risk, and that if she had known, she would not have consented to the procedure.

- On the basis of a reasonable physician disclosure standard, she lost the case and then appealed.

- The New Jersey Supreme Court made an explicit decision to change the disclosure standard to a patient viewpoint standard in which a physician must disclose all risks that could affect the patient's decision.

- The court stated that the reasonable physician standard used in the past was not consistent with the patient's right to autonomy and self-determination.

How Much Should You Disclose?

You should know what standard your state uses to determine disclosure. What does this mean for you? If your state adheres to a reasonable physician standard, your disclosure requirements might be lighter. If a patient viewpoint standard is in effect, you probably will have to disclose more information. The state medical society may be a good resource for learning about your state's laws and its interpretation.

Even if a reasonable physician standard applies, you may want to consider disclosing risks and benefits based on what a reasonable person in your patient's position would want to know. Going beyond the minimum requirements that apply to you might be more time consuming, but it could protect you:

- State court interpretations of the law can change, as in the previous New Jersey case.

- A more thorough discussion of risks and benefits could ensure that your patient has more reasonable expectations about the outcome of treatment.

- If the patient does have a complication, she might be less likely to file a claim against you if she knew the risks of a complication beforehand.

Obtaining Informed Consent

You may be accustomed to thinking of informed consent as the form a patient signs before she can have surgery. Valid, effective informed consent is not a form, it is a process. The purpose of informed consent is to ensure that a patient makes the health care decision that is right for her.

Consent is meaningful only if your patient fully understands the risks and benefits of the recommended treatment, as well as alternatives to treatment. Few, if any, patients can gain this understanding simply by reading and signing a form, regardless of how detailed it is. The following points are key:

- Nothing replaces the face-to-face discussion you have with your patient.

- Both patient and physician must participate in the discussion actively in order for it to be effective and meaningful.

- You must make a good faith effort to be sure you provide the information the patient needs, encourage her to ask questions, and answer those questions.

State requirements for informed consent vary greatly. At a minimum, though, your patient needs to know the following:

- Her diagnosis or medical condition that is prompting the treatment

- The treatment you are recommending and its purpose

- The likely benefits of the treatment

- The relative probability that the treatment will succeed

- The risks and complications the treatment could involve

- Available alternatives to your recommended treatment and their relative risks and benefits

- Possible consequences of forgoing treatment

You must inform the patient about all treatment options regardless of their cost or her insurance coverage. Remember that your duty to obtain informed consent is not limited to major surgery or hospital procedures. You also should follow the principles of the informed consent process when recommending office procedures, ordering diagnostic tests, and prescribing medications.

A patient's ability to understand the information you provide depends on many factors:

- Maturity

- Mental status and mental acuity

- Education

- Cultural background

- Willingness and ability to ask questions and actively participate in the discussion

You cannot change a patient's background or personality, but you can make an effort to structure your informed consent discussions in a way that takes each patient's individual circumstances into account. Having a meaningful informed consent discussion will be easier if you have already developed a pattern of effective communication with your patient. Strategies for effective physician–patient communication are discussed in Chapter 7, "Patient Communication."

The following suggestions may be helpful in the informed consent process:

- Include family members and significant others in the discussion if the patient wants them there.
- Use words your patient can understand. Speak in plain language, not medical jargon.
- Make sure the patient understands what you have said. Ask her to explain to you in her own words to confirm her understanding.
- Use printed educational materials, audiovisual materials, or other tools as appropriate. Be aware, though, that recent research suggests that use of multimedia materials and lengthy written materials are of limited help in increasing patients' understanding.
- Allow enough time for questions.
- Give truthful answers about your expertise, qualifications, and education.
- Base your discussion of risks and benefits on current data and guidelines.
- Never guarantee success or suggest in any way that a specific outcome is certain.

Use the informed consent checklist in Appendix E, "Professional Liability and Risk Management Check-ups," to evaluate your process.

If you are a resident, an attending physician may ask you to obtain a patient's consent. If the patient has questions that you cannot answer, be sure to consult with the supervising physician.

A thorough informed consent process can benefit both patient and physician. When the patient participates in decision making, she can be more confident that she is making the right choice and may feel better about her care. You can be reassured that the patient has a realistic understanding of the treatment you recommended and its risks and benefits.

Informed Refusal

A patient has the right to refuse to undergo treatment or diagnostic procedures you recommend. She may decide not to follow your recommendations for a variety of reasons:

- Cultural or religious beliefs
- Personal preference
- Comfort

Her evaluation of the risks and benefits may differ from yours; or she may not fully understand the possible consequences of refusing treatment. If a patient is reluctant to follow the care plan you recommended, discuss the following with her:

- Review with her your reasons for recommending the care.

- Ask the patient to explain her understanding of your recommendation.

- Ask why she is refusing the care. You may be able to clear up a misunderstanding or allay her fears.

- Make sure she understands the risks of forgoing treatment.

If a patient refuses care or chooses an alternative treatment, in all but very rare circumstances, you must respect her decision. Take the following steps to protect yourself in the event of a medical professional liability claim:

- Carefully document your discussion, including risks and benefits of treatment, alternatives to treatment, and the risks of not having the recommended treatment.

- Include the patient's reasons for refusing your recommendations.

- Be sure your documentation can demonstrate clearly that refusal was informed—that your patient fully understood the risks of rejecting your recommendations.

Special Informed Consent Rules

Your obligation to obtain informed consent and the patient's right to consent to or refuse medical treatment apply in all but a few specific circumstances:

- Emergencies
- Care provided to minors
- Court-authorized treatment

Emergencies

In a bona fide emergency you can provide care without obtaining a patient's explicit consent. If the situation is truly an emergency, the patient's consent is implied. In other words, the law assumes that the patient would consent to treatment if she could. Emergency care without consent can be provided in the following circumstances:

- The patient must be unconscious or incapable of providing an informed consent.

- Her life or health must be at serious risk unless you provide immediate medical treatment.

Good documentation is essential when you provide emergency care without a patient's explicit consent. Be sure you clearly describe the following in the medical record:

- The patient's condition
- The reasons she was unable to provide consent

- The circumstances of the emergency

- Your reasons for providing the immediate medical treatment

Minors

In general, a minor cannot consent to medical care. Her parent or legal guardian must give informed consent on her behalf. Although your minor patient cannot consent to treatment, like any other patient she is entitled to be fully informed about her care to the extent of her ability to understand.

Many states have laws that provide some exceptions, granting minors the right to consent to treatment in some circumstances. These exceptions vary greatly from state to state:

- Minors above a certain age may be able to consent to any treatment.

- Minors may be able to consent to certain types of treatment (eg, prenatal care).

- Minors above a certain age may be able to consent to certain types of treatment.

- Laws may define circumstances under which a minor is considered "emancipated" and able to consent on her own behalf.

In most states, though, the law does not address every situation in which a minor might seek or need care without a parent's consent. You should know what the law does specify in your state.

Court-Authorized Treatment

In some cases a patient may refuse treatment she needs to save her life or, if she is pregnant, her fetus' life. In these circumstances, the patient often has religious or ethical reasons for refusing treatment. For pregnant patients, ACOG's Committee on Ethics offers the following guidance:

- Make all reasonable efforts to protect the fetus, but respect the pregnant woman's autonomy.

- Remember that your role is to help the patient weigh the risks and benefits.

- Recognize the uncertainty and possibility for error in all medical care.

- Call on resources such as a hospital or institutional ethics committee to help you and the patient.

- Use the court system to resolve the dilemma only as a last resort.

Careful documentation of your discussions with the patient, her concerns about treatment, and your efforts to resolve the situation is very important in such situations.

Documenting Informed Consent

Part of the informed consent process is documenting evidence that the patient consented to treatment. You might typically document informed consent with a printed form the patient signs. States differ in their requirements:

- Some states recognize a signed consent form as a presumption that the patient provided valid consent; the plaintiff can challenge this presumption in court.

- Other states use a signed consent form as just one piece of evidence of consent.

If you develop an informed consent form for a procedure you do frequently, have an attorney who is familiar with your state's informed consent requirements review it.

Typically, informed consent is documented in one of three ways, depending on state law and, for hospital procedures, your hospital's policies:

1. The long form contains all relevant information about risks, benefits, and alternatives, as well as information specific to the individual patient.

2. The short form does not include details, but indicates that risks, benefits, and alternatives were disclosed and discussed.

3. Notes in the medical record can describe the informed consent discussion.

When documenting informed consent in the medical record, you can include:

- All information provided

- Details of the risks, benefits, and alternatives discussed

- The patient's questions and your answers

- Reference to any written materials or other patient education tools used

- Names of witnesses, if any

You should be familiar with your state's requirements and hospital policies for documenting informed consent. Do not rely only on notes in the medical record if your state requires a signed, written authorization from the patient.

Devoting the effort needed to have thorough, meaningful informed consent discussions with your patients is among the most important steps you take to reduce your medical professional liability risk. Failing to obtain informed consent may not be among the most frequent reasons for medical liability claims against ob-gyns. However, the issues discussed in the informed consent process—expected outcome, risks, and possible complications—are at the heart of many medical liability claims. By helping your patient make an informed decision that is right for her, you may reduce the chance you will be sued or enhance your defense if you are sued.

If you develop an informed consent form for a procedure you do frequently, have an attorney who is familiar with your state's informed consent requirements review it.

KEY POINTS

✓ Informed consent is a discussion, not a form.

✓ You have an affirmative duty to obtain informed consent.

✓ If you ask your patient only to read and sign a form, you have not met your obligation.

✓ Providing medical care without valid informed consent can violate a patient's rights.

✓ Standards for informed consent vary. Learn and comply with your state's requirements.

Chapter 5

Risk Management

Practicing obstetrics and gynecology is an inherently risky venture. You cannot control all risks. In spite of your best efforts, things can and do go wrong. The risks of many adverse outcomes, though, can be reduced. Learning to manage and reduce risk will improve the care your patients receive and may reduce your exposure to medical professional liability claims.

The risk management literature is extensive, and you will never exhaust the opportunities to do more to manage risk and improve your patients' safety. This chapter will introduce basic principles of risk management for obstetrics and gynecology. Topics include:

- Risk management goals and principles

- Creating a risk management–friendly environment

- Risk management strategies for the ob-gyn office

- Risk management strategies for ob-gyn services in the hospital

- Risk management and responsibilities for follow-up

- Risk management issues for residents

Risk Management Goals and Principles

The overriding goals for implementing risk management strategies in your daily practice should be to improve the quality of medical care and ensure the safety of your patients. In addition, risk management aims to reduce the risk that you will be successfully sued for medical professional liability by:

- Reducing the chances for an error in patient care

- Improving the likelihood that treatment will produce the desired results

- Increasing the odds for a successful defense if you are sued

At its most effective, risk management is not a program. It is a comprehensive approach to practice and a way of thinking. Whether you are a resident in training or an ob-gyn in practice, you should work to make risk management part of routine practice.

The overriding goals for implementing risk management strategies in your daily practice should be to improve the quality of medical care and ensure the safety of your patients.

Among the most powerful risk management tools available to you are good communication skills.

Incorporating risk management into your day-to-day routine means always being alert to opportunities to identify and address risks. Take a look around you as you go through a typical workday. Chances are you will see more than a few potential risks:

- Are there hazardous conditions that could increase the chances of patients or staff injuring themselves?

- Are laboratory results missing from a patient's chart?

- Did you have difficulty reading or understanding someone else's notes in a patient's chart?

- Did a nurse or other health care provider misunderstand your orders?

These are examples of situations that could contribute to poor outcomes and have the potential to become a medical liability claim. A risk management mind-set identifies potential areas of risk and sees those risks as opportunities to improve patient care.

Creating a Risk Management–Friendly Environment

Some of the most serious—and most preventable—errors in patient care happen because of poor communication among members of the health care team. A nurse misunderstood a physician's hastily scrawled order. Someone forgot to update the patient's chart. The list of communication blunders you have encountered probably could go on and on. Among the most powerful risk management tools available to you are good communication skills, including the following:

- Listen carefully to verbal reports from office staff, nurses, and other physicians. Confirm that you understand by verbally summarizing what you have been told, if necessary.

- Be sure others have understood your verbal orders and reports. Ask them to summarize or repeat if you are unsure. Also put verbal reports in writing for the medical record.

- Do not assume that "no news is good news." Ask if there is anything else you need to know.

- Make sure your written notes and orders are clear and legible.

- Document so that another physician could pick up the patient's care where you stopped, if necessary. (See Chapter 8, "Medical Records and Documentation.")

- If you cannot read what someone else has written in the patient's chart, ask for clarification.

Even though you, as the physician, bear primary responsibility for the patient's welfare, risk management is everyone's job. Create an atmosphere for risk management:

- Empower those around you to take responsibility for risk management.

- Make it clear that you will listen to anyone who raises an issue about a risk to patient safety.

- Ask for suggestions for reducing risks and improving safety from everyone who has contact with patients.

If you are a resident, you might feel that you have limited opportunities to affect the atmosphere for risk management. You should make the most of the chances you do have:

- Be open and approachable if nurses or other hospital staff want to discuss patient safety concerns.

- Ask your chief resident or program director to strengthen your program's risk management training.

- Get to know your institution's risk management staff.

Involving yourself in risk management activities as a resident will make the risk management approach to practice seem natural to you and will serve you well when you begin practice.

Risk Management Strategies for the Ob-Gyn Office

Incidents that trigger medical professional liability claims often begin in the office even when the event does not occur there. Also, as the trend toward performing more procedures on an outpatient basis continues, the importance of integrating risk management into your office will grow. Effective risk management in the office should address:

- The physical environment

- Personnel

- Appointment scheduling

- "New-patient" procedures

- Telephone calls

- Documentation and records management

Physical Environment

Your office's appearance and atmosphere influence patients' experiences and their perceptions about the quality of care you provide. Consider the following:

- Is the reception area pleasant and comfortable?

- Is there a private area for confidential conversations, such as financial discussions?

- Can patients overhear telephone calls or nurses' and doctors' conversations about other patients?

- Is the office clean and neat? Review all areas, including examination rooms and bathrooms.

- Are controlled substances and prescription pads secure or in a secure location?

Some aspects of your office physical environment can expose you to ordinary liability risks, not just medical liability claims:

- Are there hazards that increase the chance that patients or employees could injure themselves? For example, are stairs lacking safety rails?

- Is your office accessible to patients with disabilities? (See Chapter 12, "Government Requirements Affecting Medical Practice.")

- Are you in compliance with all relevant fire and safety codes?

If you perform even the simplest procedures in the office, you must be sure you are adequately prepared to cope with complications that might reasonably be expected to result (eg, a severe allergic reaction to an injection). To be prepared, you should:

- Have emergency equipment available that is appropriate for the range of services you provide

- Have a schedule for regular testing and maintenance of medical equipment

- Have all staff trained to respond appropriately to an emergency

(See "Professional Liability and Risk Management Check–up" in Appendix E [hereinafter referred to as Appendix E] for checklist, "Risk Management in the Office Setting.")

Personnel

From scheduling her first appointment to paying her bill, a patient may have as much contact with your office staff as she does with you. Your staff's caring attitudes and competent performance can enhance patients' experiences and reduce the threat of liability claims. However, staff insensitivity or mistakes can lead to medical professional liability claims. You are responsible for what your staff members do, so make sure they help your risk management efforts:

- Train all staff to treat patients with empathy and respect.

- Develop clear descriptions of job responsibilities to ensure that important patient care tasks are not missed.

- Delegate patient care responsibilities carefully. Consider an employee's abilities and credentials.

- Ensure that licensed employees (eg, nurses, sonographers) perform only duties within the scope of their licenses.

- Do not delegate tasks requiring clinical judgment to unqualified staff.

- Educate staff about risk management and medical liability issues.

Your staff are critical members of your risk management team. You must establish an atmosphere in which every staff member feels responsible for reducing risks and protecting patients' safety:

- Encourage your staff to identify risks and propose strategies for managing risk. Reward this behavior.

- Listen carefully when a staff member raises a concern or makes a suggestion. Take it seriously.

- Include risk management as a regular agenda item for staff meetings.

- Provide feedback and progress reports when you implement new risk management strategies.

(See Appendix E checklist, "Working With Nonphysicians," for suggested risk management techniques for nonphysician staff.)

Appointment Scheduling

No one likes to wait. Doing your best to see patients on time is not just a matter of common courtesy. It is also a useful risk management strategy. A patient who is angry and dissatisfied because of a long wait could be too anxious and irritated to provide the information you need to make an accurate diagnosis. She might also be more likely to file a medical liability claim in the event of an adverse outcome because she feels that you did not treat her courteously.

For a busy ob-gyn, some delays and schedule disruptions are unavoidable, but there are some things you can do to keep your schedule under control:

- Be realistic in setting your schedule. For example, allow enough time for travel between practice locations, for returning urgent calls between patient visits, and the like.

- Instruct staff to let patients know if you are running behind schedule. Have them offer to reschedule appointments if the delay will be lengthy.

- Designate a staff member to monitor how long patients have been waiting.

- Pay attention to the patient's appointment time and the time you actually see her. If she has been waiting, apologize for the delay.

Periodically monitor waiting times in your office. If you find that you are always behind schedule or patients often wait for a long time, make some changes. Seeing patients on time will improve their views of the care they receive and could reduce your chances of being sued.

Handling New Patients

New patients require more time and effort. The initial encounter is critical to building an effective physician–patient relationship. A risk management approach to handling new patients will help to make sure you do not miss information crucial to providing her care:

- If the patient's previous records are available, review them before you meet with her.

- If possible, try to meet with a new patient in your private office (if you have one). This setting may make her feel more at ease and encourage her to provide a thorough history.

- If possible, obtain a new patient's history through a personal interview instead of having her complete forms if you can. You will be better able to get additional details, and your questions may prompt the patient's memory for important facts.

- If you have the patient complete a history form or delegate history taking to a staff member, be sure to review the history with the patient.

New patients need to be oriented to your practice, whether you are a resident in a busy outpatient clinic or an ob-gyn in private practice. You may decide to delegate this task to staff or develop written materials. Make sure new patients know:

- How to contact you during and after office hours

- Covering arrangements with other physicians

- Hospitals you use

- What to do in an emergency

- Practice policies regarding bills, copayment/coinsurance, missed appointments, and other administrative issues

- The range of services you provide

It is probably wise to provide this information periodically to established patients, too, especially if information changes.

Telephone Calls

Telephone calls frequently are a key element of a medical professional liability claim. Be aware of the following:

- Providing any medical advice over the telephone, whether you or a non-physician practice employee provides the advice, is considered medical care.

- Courts have found that providing medical advice over the telephone establishes a physician–patient relationship and the duty to provide services meeting the standard of care.

- You are liable for any advice provided by anyone in your practice.

You could virtually eliminate the liability risk connected with telephone calls by refusing to provide advice over the telephone. For most ob-gyns, though, this strategy is probably not feasible. If you do provide medical advice by telephone, you should develop specific, written procedures that staff must follow in handling phone calls:

- Include questions to be asked of every caller.

- Provide instructions for when to immediately refer calls to a physician and when to instruct patients to go immediately to the hospital or call emergency medical services.

- Provide instructions about when you should be interrupted to take a call.

- Make it easy for patients to speak with you. Set a low threshold for referring calls to a physician.

- Instruct staff to answer calls quickly and politely. Provide a time when you will return the call.

- Do not permit nonclinical staff to triage phone calls or give advice.

- Train staff periodically on telephone procedures and document the training.

Take a risk management approach to your telephone conversations with patients:

- Make sure the patient understands what you have told her and agrees to follow your instructions before ending the conversation. If in doubt, have her repeat your instructions.

- Always provide instructions about what she should do if symptoms continue or get worse. Be certain she knows when she should call you again, schedule an appointment, or get immediate medical attention.

- Do not provide medical advice over the telephone to patients you do not know.

- Exercise caution in prescribing over the telephone. Be familiar with your state's laws on telephone prescribing.

Include in the patient's medical record notes from all telephone calls. Documenting telephone calls in patients' medical records may seem burdensome, especially during a long night on call. An accurate record of what you discussed will be important the next time you see the patient, and it could prove crucial to your defense of a liability claim. Telephone notes should include the following information:

- Date and time of the call

- Patient's complaints or symptoms

- Advice provided, including advice about when to seek care

The following suggestions will make the task of documenting telephone calls a little easier:

- Provide staff with a standard template for documenting calls. It might be helpful to use a form that includes spaces for the necessary elements, not just a "While You Were Out" slip.

Make it easy for patients to speak with you. Set a low threshold for referring calls to a physician.

- Develop a similar template for your own use.

- Consider dictating notes from telephone calls handled out of the office.

Telephone courtesy also should be part of your risk management plan for telephone calls. If your office telephones are not answered promptly or if callers are put on hold for long periods, patients may become frustrated. An overburdened telephone system could create delays or barriers to patients trying to contact you with urgent or emergency problems. Consider the following strategies for ensuring that patients who call are treated courteously:

- Set a limit for how long office staff can allow the telephone to ring.

- Limit the length of time a patient can remain on hold.

- Monitor the volume of calls to determine when the office needs additional telephone lines.

Chaperones

Regardless of your sex, as a physician you are vulnerable to false charges of sexual misconduct or inappropriate behavior in the examination room. Because of the nature of the services ob-gyns provide, they are at particular risk. Patients sometimes misunderstand pelvic examinations or procedures like vaginal ultrasonography. To protect yourself and reassure your patients, establish these procedures:

- Take time to explain any procedure or examination you will perform and why you are doing it.

- Have a chaperone present in the examination or procedure room to reassure the patient and to serve as a witness if any charges of inappropriate conduct are made.

- If you are a resident, follow your program's requirements or guidelines on using chaperones.

Documentation and Records Management

Practicing careful documentation and records management reduces your exposure to medical professional liability claims and damages in multiple ways. For example:

- A careful, thorough, legible medical record can help improve patient care and reduce the chances of error.

- If you are sued, careful, thorough, legible documentation that you met the standard of care will be your best defense.

Proper documentation is so important to medical liability and risk management that this book devotes a separate chapter to the topic (see Chapter 8, "Medical Records and Documentation"). For a risk management approach to managing records, consider the following:

- Do you complete, date, and sign chart notes promptly?

- Can you find a patient's medical record when you need it?

- Do you have a system for flagging charts awaiting laboratory or diagnostic test results or keeping such charts in a designated place?

- Are completed charts filed promptly?

- Do physicians in the practice keep all charts in the office?

- Are risk assessment and screening tools (eg, prenatal risk assessments) kept with and attached securely to the chart?

- Do you promptly review and sign all laboratory results before they are placed in a patient's chart and filed?

- Are records of telephone calls and copies of patient e-mails kept with the chart?

(See Appendix E checklist, "Medical Records and Documentation," for other helpful suggestions.)

Risk Management Strategies for Ob-Gyn Services in the Hospital

You are most likely to be sued for medical professional liability in connection with events that happen in the hospital. Reducing risks in the hospital setting involves:

- Preparing the patient for her hospital stay

- Following hospital risk management policies and protocols and participating in their development

- Consulting and communicating with other physicians and members of the patient's health care team

(See Appendix E checklist, "Risk Management in the Hospital," for other helpful suggestions.)

Preparing the Patient

Begin thinking about risk management for the hospital patient before you admit her to the hospital. Thoroughly discuss the following with her:

- The reason for her admission to the hospital

- Any procedures you recommend she have

- Alternatives to hospital treatment

- Risks and potential complications of hospital care

- Her expected length of stay in the hospital

The informed consent process is a keystone of risk management (see Chapter 4, "Informed Consent"). Make sure your patient understands that things might not go as planned. She could have a surgical complication or a hospital-acquired infection, for example. If she understands that these are risks of treatment, she may be less likely to sue if she has a complication.

Carefully review the chart each time you see your patient in the hospital. Verify orders and review notes from nurses, residents, and other physicians.

Let the patient and her family know what to expect during her hospital stay. She will be less anxious and better prepared to participate in her care. For example, make sure she knows:

- When and how often you typically conduct rounds

- How to contact you

- What other physicians (eg, consultants, your partners, covering physicians) will be involved in her care

- Whether residents and medical students will be present in the hospital and involved in her care

While your patient is in the hospital, her medical record will be your main method for communicating with others who are involved in her care. Close attention to accurate and complete transfer of records, as well as close monitoring of the chart during your patient's hospital stay, are critical to risk management and may reduce the likelihood of an error. Communication in this setting includes:

- Copy and send all risk assessment forms to the hospital before the patient arrives.

- Flag the record of a high-risk patient (for example, a patient with co-morbidities) so that hospital staff will be aware of conditions that might require extra attention.

- Be sure to update prenatal records to include visits or test results that happen after the transfer.

- Include any risk assessment forms or checklists in the transfer of prenatal records.

- Follow hospital rules for reviewing, updating, and signing patient charts.

- Carefully review the chart each time you see your patient in the hospital. Verify orders and review notes from nurses, residents, and other physicians.

Following the Hospital's Risk Management Procedures

Your hospital probably has a formal risk management program staffed by risk management professionals. The hospital's risk management policies are in place to protect your patients, and they can help protect you. Failing to follow the hospital's procedures could be interpreted as violating the standard of care. The following suggestions will help you avoid this:

- Become familiar with the hospital's risk management protocols and policies.

- Get to know the risk management staff.

- Comply with all hospital risk management policies.

- Take advantage of any opportunities to participate in the review and design of your hospital's quality assurance and risk management programs.

Communication and Consultation With Other Physicians and Health Care Professionals

When your patient is hospitalized, you are only one of many people caring for her. Nurses, medical assistants, laboratory and other technologists, and other physicians may be involved. You can be held liable for the actions of others—even hospital employees. Two legal doctrines apply:

1. Under the *borrowed servant* doctrine you can be held liable for the negligent actions of someone else's employee, such as a labor and delivery nurse, when he or she works under your direction.

2. Under the *captain-of-the-ship* doctrine, you are responsible for the actions of everyone under your supervision and control—for example, members of the surgical team when you are the primary surgeon.

Take reasonable precautions to protect yourself against others' negligence:

- Make sure you adequately communicate with and supervise other health care professionals who come into contact with your patients.

- Be sure you know the capabilities and legal scope of practice for hospital staff to whom you delegate duties.

- If you delegate duties to someone unqualified to perform them, you could be found to be negligent in a medical professional liability claim.

Obstetrician–gynecologists frequently encounter complex patient care situations that call for the skills and expertise of another physician. Delaying or mishandling referrals and consultation requests can leave you exposed to medical liability claims if the patient experiences an adverse outcome. Do not delay asking for a consultation or making a referral when the patient would benefit from another physician's skills and knowledge. Juries have little patience with a physician's reluctance to ask for help when the patient needs it.

The involvement of multiple physicians in a patient's hospital care can lead to confusion. The patient and her family may become anxious and might be uncomfortable with another physician. Nursing staff may be unsure who is in charge, what orders to follow, and whom to contact about the patient. Take the following precautions:

- Make sure the patient and her family know that another physician will become involved in her care.

- Notify hospital staff about a consulting physician and his or her role.

- Provide specific instructions about who is in charge of the patient's care and who can write orders.

- If you are a resident, be sure you understand the roles and responsibilities of consulting physicians who see your patients. Ask the attending physician for clarification if necessary.

(For further risk management suggestions regarding your interactions with other physicians, see Appendix E checklist, "Working With Other Physicians.")

In some instances you might refer a patient's care to another physician. Even when you have decided that another physician is better qualified to care for your patient, do not drop out of the picture. Your patient should not feel that you have abandoned her:

- Discuss with the patient your reasons for wanting another physician to take over her care.

- Obtain her consent to the transfer of care and document it in her record.

- Continue to monitor her care and progress to the extent practical. Ask the other physician to keep you informed.

- If she is admitted to your hospital, stop by to see her.

An appropriate level of continuing involvement in the care of a patient you referred to another physician can have several benefits. The patient probably will feel more comfortable with the care she is receiving and will appreciate your interest in her welfare. She may receive better care because of the additional oversight. If there is a complication or adverse outcome, your patient may be less likely to sue or to name you in a claim.

Working With Residents

If you have privileges at a teaching hospital, residents may be involved in caring for your patients. Apply the same risk management approach to working with residents that you do to working with other members of the health care team, but also keep these points in mind:

- Introduce the resident to your patient and explain his or her role.

- Make sure you are familiar with the resident's level of training and qualifications. Delegating tasks to a resident who has not been fully trained to perform them exposes your patients to potential harm and exposes you to increased liability.

- Be clear and specific in communicating with the resident.

- Remember that the resident may have more direct contact with the patient than you do. Make sure he or she has all necessary information. Your patient will lose confidence in her care if the resident seems not to know what is going on.

- Notify the resident about any consultations, tests, or procedures you have ordered. The resident can then ensure that your orders are carried out and that results are recorded in the chart.

- Let the resident know when you want to be contacted about your patients. Stress that if in doubt, she or he should not hesitate to contact you.

- Make sure your response to a resident who calls you with questions or concerns about a patient reinforces what you have said about when to contact you. If you berate a resident who calls you when you think it is unnecessary, he or she may be reluctant to call you when you are needed.

- Always read and review the resident's notes in the chart. Do not assume the chart is correct. Note and discuss with the resident any errors or disagreements.

- Follow insurers' rules about billing for care that a resident provides under your supervision.

Risk Management and Responsibilities for Follow-up

Whose responsibility is it to see that a patient gets her mammogram, visits the consultant you recommended, has blood work done, or comes back for a repeat Pap test? Do not learn the hard way that most juries would consider it your responsibility, not the patient's.

Your duty to provide care extends to making reasonable efforts to ensure that the patient receives the care you recommended. What is a reasonable follow-up effort? It varies depending on the circumstances. In general, the more serious the condition and the patient's symptoms, the more intensive your follow-up should be. As the physician, you are in a far better position than the patient to understand the importance of complying with your recommendations.

Every ob-gyn should have systems in place to ensure appropriate follow-up for the following:

- Laboratory tests and diagnostic procedures

- Consultations and referrals

- Return appointments

Laboratory Tests and Diagnostic Procedures

Failing to follow-up on abnormal laboratory and diagnostic test results can have serious consequences for a patient's health. If a patient's infection or cervical cancer is undiagnosed because the test results did not come back from the laboratory or were filed away before you could take action, you will have no good excuse to offer a jury if you are sued. A useful guideline is that if you believe a test or diagnostic procedure is important enough to justify the cost, possible discomfort, and inconvenience to the patient, it is important enough to follow-up.

How can a busy practice keep track of all the tests and procedures you order? An effective solution can be as simple as an inexpensive paper and pencil log system. For example, you could direct your staff to:

- List all tests ordered in a notebook, by date.

- Check entries off as results come in and are forwarded to you for review.

- At a set interval (eg, every 2 weeks), review the log for results that are past due.

- If test results are missing, contact the facility to see if the test was done.

- If the test was not done, contact the patient to remind her to have the test done.

- Document all follow-up on missing results in the patient's chart.

Other methods that have worked for some practices include placing all patient charts awaiting test results in a central location for periodic staff review and follow-up. Also, some electronic medical record or medical office management systems include features for tracking tests and procedures.

The tracking system that is right for your practice is the one you will use consistently. If a tracking system is too complicated or burdensome, it will not be effective. Having a system you do not use consistently could be more damaging to the defense of a medical professional liability claim than not having one at all. Talk with other physicians, practice management consultants, or software vendors to identify effective and efficient tracking systems. Your medical liability insurance carrier might be a helpful resource. Practice management journals and consultants also can provide information.

Tracking your practice's laboratory test and diagnostic procedure results can be a challenge, but at least it is under your control. Ensuring that patients actually have the tests and procedures you order may be an even greater challenge. Here are a few suggestions:

- Provide a written information sheet including the name of the test, location of the facility, and any pretest instructions (eg, full bladder for abdominal ultrasonography).

- Explain carefully why you are ordering the test (eg, to screen for breast cancer) and what she can expect.

- Include a brief explanation of the importance of the test to your patient's health on the information sheet.

- Document in the patient's record the information you have provided.

Taking reasonable steps to make sure the patient understands the importance of the tests you order may improve patient compliance. It also could help protect you in the event of a medical liability claim.

Consultations and Referrals

In the typical busy ob-gyn practice, it may be easy to lose track of whether reports you expect from consulting physicians arrive. If you do not see the consultant's report, you cannot act on the consultant's advice and provide the right care for your patient. Of course, if your patient does not follow up on your recommendation for a referral or consultation, you will never get the advice. Either of these situations could expose you to medical professional liability risk.

Consider some of the following fairly simple steps to reduce the risk of not receiving critical information from another physician:

- Explain to the patient why you are referring her to another physician and the importance of promptly following through on the referral.

- Be specific about whether the other physician will be taking over her care or whether the other physician will be making recommendations to you, which you will discuss with her at another visit.

- Have your staff make the appointment for her before she leaves your office.

- If you are expecting a report from a consultant, flag the chart.

- Maintain a log of consultations and referrals. Have staff follow up on missing consultant reports.

If a patient does not keep her referral appointment or a consultant fails to communicate with you, you will be able to demonstrate that you took reasonable steps to ensure that your patient received appropriate care.

Return Appointments

It is likely that several times a day you tell your patients to come back to see you within some specified time. You may believe it is each patient's responsibility to return at the recommended interval, but you could be held liable for not providing needed follow-up care when the patient failed to come back as recommended. Patients have argued successfully that if they had known the importance of the follow-up care, they would have obtained it.

How can you protect yourself from this type of allegation? First, make sure you tell patients clearly and specifically why you want them to return and what could happen if they do not. Then, take reasonable steps to ensure that patients comply:

- Schedule a patient's return appointments before she leaves the office.

- Schedule postoperative and postpartum visits before you discharge a patient from the hospital.

- Designate a staff member to follow-up on missed appointments every day.

- If a patient with a potentially serious condition does not return for follow–up care after a telephone reminder, consider sending a certified letter with return receipt requested.

- Document all follow-up efforts in the patient's chart.

Risk Management Issues for Residents

If you are currently completing an ob-gyn residency, now is an excellent time to begin incorporating a risk management approach into your daily practice rou-

You may believe it is the patient's responsibility to return at the recommended interval, but you could be held liable for not providing needed follow-up care when the patient failed to come back as recommended.

tines. All points discussed so far in this chapter are relevant for residents, either now or when you enter practice. A few points deserve special emphasis:

- Make sure the attending physician knows your level of training and qualifications.

- If an attending physician asks you to perform a procedure for which you have not yet been fully trained, speak up.

- Familiarize yourself with your program's risk management guidelines, documentation requirements, and other protocols.

One of the many difficult situations you face as a resident is when to contact the attending physician about a change in your patient's status. These conflicting thoughts are probably familiar:

- You are concerned about the patient and want to do the right thing.

- You want to learn to rely on your own judgment and know the attending wants you to learn this too.

- You are reluctant to interrupt the attending physician at home or in the office.

Take a risk management approach to these situations. If you are in doubt about whether you should notify the attending physician, make the call. If he or she thinks you called unnecessarily, you may be embarrassed for a while. Your attending physician may even be angry. But if you do not call and your skills and knowledge are not adequate to help the patient, she could suffer serious and unnecessary harm.

Beginning now to see your daily routines as well as emergency situations through a risk management lens may reduce the chances that you will be named in a medical professional liability case during residency. It also will prepare you for practice in the years ahead.

KEY POINTS

✓ The goal of risk management is improving care and preventing harm.

✓ Risk management cannot prevent all medical professional liability claims, but it can improve chances for your defense.

✓ Risk management works best as a comprehensive approach to practice, not a separate activity.

✓ Good communication with patients and the health care team is a powerful risk management tool.

✓ A thorough informed consent process and strong documentation practices are cornerstones of risk management.

✓ Risk management is everybody's job.

Chapter 6

High-Risk Areas for Litigation in Obstetrics and Gynecology

Being sued for medical professional liability is common for ob-gyns. More than three quarters of ACOG Fellows who responded to the 2006 ACOG Survey on Professional Liability had been sued (see Wilson N, Strunk AL. Overview of the 2006 ACOG Survey on Professional Liability. ACOG Clin Rev 2007;12[2]:1, 13–6). On average, responding ob-gyns had experienced 2.6 claims during their careers. It is important to realize that some activities within the scope of ob-gyn practice generate more medical liability claims than others. Knowing what the high-risk areas are can help you focus your risk management efforts on the practice activities that put you most at risk of being sued.

This chapter will identify and describe several areas of practice that generate large numbers of medical liability claims, including:

- The neurologically impaired infant and stillbirth or neonatal death

- Delivery methods

- Failure to diagnose

- Laparoscopy

The data you will see are from the 2006 ACOG Survey on Professional Liability. The 2006 survey is the ninth in a series of surveys of ACOG Fellows on medical liability issues. The data represent the experiences of 10,659 ACOG member physicians. The results include data on medical liability claims opened or closed between 2003 and 2005.

Obstetric care is the source of more medical liability claims than gynecologic services, and obstetric claims are more expensive:

- Of claims reported, 62.1% were related to obstetrics.

- Damages paid in obstetric cases averaged $651,300; gynecologic claims, $237,107.

Why does obstetric practice generate so many more medical liability claims? Several factors probably contribute:

- Astonishing improvements in pregnancy outcomes for both mothers and babies create expectations for a perfect outcome with every pregnancy.

Almost one third (30.8%) of obstetric claims involved a neurologically impaired infant, and 15.8% involved a stillbirth or neonatal death.

- Parents of an infant who dies or has a congenital defect experience tremendous emotional distress, grief, and guilt. Looking for answers may turn into looking for someone to blame.

- The financial burden of caring for a disabled child can be overwhelming for many young families.

The Neurologically Impaired Infant and Stillbirth or Neonatal Death

Two primary allegations accounted for almost half of all obstetric claims. Almost one third (30.8%) of obstetric claims involved a neurologically impaired infant, and 15.8% involved a stillbirth or neonatal death. Little has changed since 1983 when ACOG first surveyed its members about medical professional liability issues. At that time, 31% of obstetric claims involved a neurologically impaired infant and 15% involved a stillbirth or neonatal death.

If you practice obstetrics and especially if you are dealing with a neurologically impaired infant claim, make sure both you and your defense team are fully aware of the current scientific understanding of brain injury in infants. Two useful resources are available:

1. *Neonatal Encephalopathy and Cerebral Palsy: Defining the Pathogenesis and Pathophysiology,* the report of ACOG's Task Force on Neonatal Encephalopathy

2. *Prenatal and Perinatal Factors Associated With Brain Disorders,* from the National Institutes of Health

Delivery Methods

Most obstetric liability claims relate to incidents that are alleged to have happened during labor and delivery. Caring for a pregnant woman in labor and during delivery often requires making rapid decisions. Events during labor can sometimes signal a difficult delivery or problems with the infant. If you are sued, the patient's attorney and scientific expert are sure to search the patient's record for any clues that labor was not going well or that you should have provided different care. Several steps can help prevent lawsuits for adverse outcomes:

- Monitor the progress of a patient in labor at appropriate intervals.

- Document carefully the progress of labor and your management of the patient.

- Obtain informed consent before performing any procedure.

- Always dictate a procedural note for difficult or operative deliveries.

- Not all maternal complications or infant problems are immediately apparent at delivery. Consider dictating a note for all deliveries, even those that seem unremarkable.

- Maintain ongoing communication with a patient about her progress of labor and your plan of management.

Cesarean Delivery

Patients who have cesarean deliveries file a disproportionately high percentage of liability claims. Approximately 26% of all live births are by cesarean delivery, but 38.8% of obstetric claims reported in the 2006 ACOG Survey on Professional Liability were cesarean deliveries. Patients who underwent cesarean delivery filed the following claims:

- 40.1% of neurologically impaired infant claims

- 40.7% of stillbirth or neonatal death claims

- 49.5% of maternal death claims

- 49.6% of major claims for maternal injury

Vaginal Birth After Cesarean Delivery

ACOG considers vaginal birth after cesarean delivery (VBAC) an appropriate option for reducing the likelihood of a repeat cesarean delivery for some patients in some circumstances. Be aware, though, of the patient care risks and liability risks. Only 4.5% of live births were by VBAC, but 5.2% of obstetric claims in the 2006 ACOG Survey on Professional Liability data involved VBAC. If you practice obstetrics, the following points are important:

- Be sure you understand the patient and facility criteria for VBAC and the contraindications to VBAC (see ACOG Practice Bulletin 54, "Vaginal Birth After Previous Cesarean Delivery").

- Discuss risks and benefits with the patient in detail.

- Document the informed consent discussion carefully.

A patient (and her health insurer) might be very anxious to avoid a repeat cesarean and could pressure you to attempt VBAC when you do not feel it is appropriate. Remember that attempting VBAC in a facility that is not properly staffed and equipped or with a patient who does not meet the criteria puts the patient and her baby at risk of serious harm. It also puts you at risk of a medical professional liability lawsuit that could be difficult to defend.

Operative Vaginal Delivery

According to ACOG Practice Bulletin 17, "Operative Vaginal Delivery," 10–15% of vaginal deliveries include using forceps or vacuum extraction. Instrumental vaginal deliveries have been associated with increased maternal and neonatal morbidity. To minimize risk:

- Be sure you are familiar with indications for using forceps and vacuum extractors as well as possible complications.

- Make sure you have the necessary skill. If you have not been fully trained to use forceps or the vacuum extractor or if your skills are rusty, do not attempt an operative vaginal delivery.

- Follow any hospital protocols for operative vaginal delivery.

Obtaining informed consent for an operative vaginal delivery is, of course, necessary. Keep in mind that a woman who may have been in labor for many hours might not be in the best position to fully understand and remember what you tell her about the risks, benefits, and alternatives. The following steps may help:

- Consider including a discussion about operative vaginal delivery in your routine prenatal information and education.

- If you discuss operative vaginal delivery or provide any educational materials in the course of prenatal care, be sure to document it in the patient's office record.

- Document informed consent to the operative vaginal delivery in the hospital chart.

- Dictate a procedural note describing the delivery.

- Alert nursery staff and the baby's physician that you used forceps or vacuum extraction.

Shoulder Dystocia

Shoulder dystocia is an obstetric emergency, threatening harm to both the patient and her baby. Respondents to the 2006 ACOG Survey on Professional Liability cited shoulder dystocia/large baby/large for gestational age as a significant factor in all cases of infant injury, including neurological impairment. Whether you are a veteran of more than 1,000 deliveries or a resident still in training, guidance for minimizing risk from shoulder dystocia is the same:

- Prepare: review and practice techniques for managing shoulder dystocia.

- Make sure you are familiar with the hospital protocol for shoulder dystocia (eg, how to summon extra help).

- When shoulder dystocia occurs, document carefully the techniques you used, any injuries that resulted, and plans for follow-up of the infant.

Induction and Augmentation of Labor

Use of oxytocic agents was a significant factor in all obstetric claims and in all claims for neurologically impaired infants. The following may be helpful:

- Be familiar with criteria and methods for labor induction (see ACOG Practice Bulletin 10, "Induction of Labor," for example).

- Discuss the risks and benefits of inducing labor and obtain informed consent.

- Document your reasons for inducing labor.

Gynecologic Claims and Failure to Diagnose

What is the primary reason, apart from obstetric care, for which ob-gyns are sued for medical professional liability? Despite the risk of patient injury and complications that is part of the surgery you perform, you are most likely to be sued because of something you did not do:

- Delay in diagnosis or failure to diagnose was the primary allegation in 29% of gynecologic claims reported in the 2006 ACOG Survey on Professional Liability.

- Damages for failure-to-diagnose claims averaged $422,557; breast cancer, $420,427; cervical cancer, $576,786; and ovarian cancer, $317,800.

Breast Cancer

Your role in providing continuing care to relatively healthy patients over many years may make you vulnerable to claims that you failed to make a timely diagnosis of breast cancer. Many of your patients probably rely on you to provide most, if not all, of their preventive care, including breast cancer screening. Your patients are also likely to consult you rather than another physician for concerns about breast pain or breast lumps.

Annual examinations and problem visits offer opportunities for early breast cancer detection, but also open up possibilities for allegations that you did not take the steps you should have taken to find breast cancer. Patient age is often a factor in claims of missed or delayed diagnosis of breast cancer.

Historically, ACOG surveys on professional liability show that nearly one third of the claims for failure to diagnose breast cancer involve a patient who was age 40 years or younger, and nearly two thirds of claims involve women younger than 50 years. The risk of breast cancer does climb steeply with age, from a 1 in 233 chance for women between ages 30 and 40 years to a 1 in 27 risk for women between ages 60 and 70 years, according to the National Cancer Institute. Do not let these statistics lull you or your younger patients into complacency about breast cancer. The following steps should be taken:

- Follow national guidelines for breast cancer screening.

- Strongly encourage patients to follow your screening recommendations. Stress that women their age can and do get breast cancer.

- Take reports of breast pain or breast lumps seriously, even if you cannot find a problem.

- Do not hesitate to refer patients for consultations or imaging studies.

- Set up a system for tracking mammogram results and other reports (see Chapter 5, "Risk Management").

- Follow up aggressively with patients who report breast symptoms to make sure they obtain recommended care.

- Document all findings, as well as all follow-up efforts.

Laparoscopy

Use of the laparoscope in gynecologic surgery continues to expand. Laparoscopy's benefits of shorter hospital stays, lower blood loss, and smaller scars come with the risk of complications and lawsuits. According to the 2006 ACOG Survey on Professional Liability, laparoscopic procedures ranked third among the primary factors involved in all gynecologic claims during the 3-year period from 2003 through 2005.

Obstetrics and gynecology is, without question, a high-risk specialty for medical professional liability claims. Some areas of practice, though, generate higher numbers of claims than others. As you work to reduce your medical liability risk, it makes sense to concentrate efforts on those clinical activities most likely to result in a claim. ACOG has developed a number of clinical practice documents that can serve as useful resources for making sure you are up-to-date with current practice in potentially risky areas such as those discussed in this chapter. Paying especially close attention to documentation and risk management interventions in these practice areas also may help to reduce your risk.

KEY POINTS

✓ Obstetric care results in approximately 62% of medical professional liability claims against ob-gyns.

✓ The most frequent allegation in obstetric claims is a neurologically impaired infant.

✓ Cesarean deliveries accounted for 39% of all obstetric claims.

✓ Failure to diagnose or delay in diagnosis was the most frequent allegation in gynecologic claims.

✓ Breast cancer was the condition cited most often in failure to diagnose claims.

Chapter 7

Patient Communication

Communicating effectively with patients is key to providing good patient care. Moreover, if an adverse outcome or incident occurs, your ability to communicate effectively, accurately, and sensitively could reduce the risk of litigation. Poor communication adds to patient dissatisfaction and frustration.

Although good physician–patient communication depends on both parties, it is your responsibility to establish an atmosphere that promotes effective communication. Your skills and sensitivity will determine whether effective communication is possible.

This chapter will discuss:

- Steps for effective communication

- Overcoming barriers to effective communication

- Communicating via e-mail

- Giving bad news: disclosing adverse outcomes and medical errors

- Terminating the physician–patient relationship

Steps for Effective Communication

Communicating with your patients in a way that both ensures good care and reduces medical professional liability risk is an ongoing process in which you:

- Lay the groundwork for an effective dialogue

- Gather and provide accurate information

- Obtain informed consent

- Stay in touch

- Follow-up

Lay the Groundwork for an Effective Dialogue

Establish the right atmosphere for effective communication by conveying a positive attitude, being respectful, and being honest. A patient's perception that a physician has a poor attitude and does not want to communicate with her contributes to some lawsuits. In contrast, a partnership between physician and

It is your responsibility to establish an atmosphere that promotes effective communication.

patient will improve medical care and can decrease the likelihood of a liability claim. Begin your efforts to establish a partnership with your patient from your first contact with her:

- Introduce yourself, sit down, and describe how you will be involved in her care.

- Make sure you are neat and well groomed at all times. Patients have little confidence in physicians with a sloppy appearance.

- Make eye contact.

- Convey a positive, caring attitude.

- Make the patient feel that taking care of her is your highest priority.

A partnership requires mutual respect. Respect your patient and treat her as a mature, intelligent human being:

- Understand and respect her beliefs.

- Ask the patient how she wants to be addressed. Do not use her first name unless she asks you to.

- Avoid being arrogant and pompous.

- Communicate at the patient's level, but do not be condescending. Speak in plain language and avoid using medical jargon.

- Explain clearly the services you will provide and make sure the patient understands what you have told her.

To communicate effectively with your patient, she must be able to trust you and trust what you are telling her. Building trust requires that you:

- Be honest with your patient.

- Establish yourself as her ally.

- Take the time to answer questions truthfully.

- If you are a resident, explain that you are a physician in training, supervised by more experienced physicians.

- Remember that patients have the right to refuse treatment by residents. You can explain the benefits of resident involvement, but you must respect the patient's ultimate decision.

Gather and Provide Accurate Information

Your ability to arrive at an accurate diagnosis and formulate an appropriate treatment plan will depend on the accuracy and completeness of the history you obtain. The patient has a responsibility to describe her symptoms and history accurately and honestly, but ob-gyn care involves issues that some women may have difficulty discussing with a stranger—you. If your patient feels comfortable, she will be more likely to provide a thorough history and to seek answers to her questions. The following techniques will help:

- Where possible, ask open-ended questions.

- Practice active listening:

  —Acknowledge your patient's emotions and needs.

  —Restate what your patient has said to confirm that you have understood her.

  —Pay attention to the nonverbal messages you send. Smiling and nodding your head, for example, can encourage open discussion, while appearing impatient or inattentive may discourage your patient from sharing her concerns or asking questions.

- Do not interrupt or finish her sentences for her.

- Allow enough time for questions and discussion.

Obtain Informed Consent

The informed consent discussions you hold with patients are a critical component of the type of collaborative, effective physician–patient communication that can decrease the risk of a professional liability claim:

- Fully explain your diagnostic findings, treatment options, your recommended treatment, benefits, risks, and alternatives. Include the risks of alternative treatment and the option of no treatment and its risks.

- Make sure your patient understands. Ask her to explain her understanding of what you told her.

It is your patient's responsibility to consider your recommendations and to weigh the benefits and disadvantages. It is her right to decide what is best for her. (Chapter 4 provides a more detailed discussion of the informed consent process.)

Stay in Touch

Although establishing effective physician–patient communication is critical, it is equally important to maintain an open dialogue with your patient throughout the duration of your relationship. Apply the same principles: be honest and respectful, encourage and answer questions, and make sure your patient understands what you have told her. The following points are important:

- Keep your patient informed about her progress. Hospitalized patients should receive daily updates; patients having office-based care should be updated at every visit.

- During annual well-woman visits, include a discussion comparing last year's visit with the current examination.

- Make sure your patient receives consistent information from all sources (resident, supervising physician, nurses). Inconsistencies are confusing and can set the stage for a lawsuit if the outcome is less than optimal.

Your communication responsibilities do not end immediately after treatment, delivery, or surgery. Complications often arise during the recovery period when the patient is at home.

Follow-up

Your communication responsibilities do not end immediately after treatment, delivery, or surgery. Complications often arise during the recovery period when the patient is at home. Provide careful, specific instructions on the following:

- What the patient should expect during the recovery period

- Possible complications and symptoms that should prompt a call to you

- Self-care

- Any activity restrictions

- Follow-up visits (ideally scheduled before the patient leaves your office or the hospital)

If possible, provide detailed written instructions for follow-up care and put a copy in the patient's record. (See Appendix E for the risk management checklist, "Patient Communication.")

Overcoming Barriers to Effective Communication

Communicating effectively in some circumstances may be a significant challenge. Cultural differences, language differences, disabilities, and limited health literacy can create barriers to communication. Your ethical obligations, common sense, and—in some cases—the law dictate that you make extra efforts to overcome those barriers.

Cultural Differences

Patients from cultures different from your own may have beliefs or practices that lead them to behave in ways that differ from what you expect. These differences might include:

- Reluctance to discuss personal health topics openly

- Reluctance to challenge an authority figure such as a doctor by asking questions

- Desire to involve extended family and friends in discussion and decision making

- Use of treatments and remedies that are traditional in the patient's culture

You cannot expect to have in-depth knowledge of all cultures, but being aware of and respectful of others' beliefs and practices is an important first step. This includes the following:

- Remember that cultural differences are not limited to race, ethnicity, or nationality.

- Be sensitive to the possibility that your patient's cultural background might affect how she communicates with you.

- Be aware of your own cultural beliefs and biases. Medicine is a culture of its own!

Limited English Proficiency

If you and your patient do not speak the same language, communication will clearly be a challenge. It is your responsibility to overcome language barriers:

- Receiving inadequate information hinders making an accurate diagnosis and planning appropriate treatment.

- You will not be able to obtain truly informed consent and set realistic expectations for treatment.

- You cannot ensure that your patient understands your instructions for self-care and follow-up.

All these factors increase the risk of an adverse outcome, misunderstanding, or a lawsuit. Consider using some of the following strategies for overcoming language barriers:

- If your community has many non-English speaking residents, hire bilingual office staff and train them to translate.

- Translate written materials (patient education materials, office forms, etc.) into languages commonly spoken by your patients or obtain materials written in those languages.

- Use telephone translation lines for patients who speak languages not commonly found in your community.

If you receive federal financial assistance (for example, you participate in Medicare, Medicaid, or other federally funded health programs), Title VI of the Civil Rights Act may require you to provide language assistance at no cost to patients with limited English proficiency (see Chapter 12, "Government Requirements Affecting Medical Practice"). Requirements will vary depending on your circumstances.

Patients with hearing impairments and other disabilities affecting communication benefit from The Americans With Disabilities Act (ADA). The ADA requires you to provide any assistance needed to communicate effectively with patients with disabilities affecting hearing, vision, or speech (see Chapter 12):

- Patients with hearing impairments might need a sign language interpreter, an assistive listening device, or teletypewriter (TTY) device.

- Patients with visual impairments might need to receive Braille or large-print versions of written materials.

- You must provide this communication assistance at no cost to the patient.

Try to determine any special communication needs and the patient's communication preferences before an office visit, if possible.

Health Literacy

A surprising number of your patients may have difficulty understanding the information they need to make health care decisions and comply with their treatment. Health literacy is the ability to understand and act on:

- Appointment notices

- Instructions for taking medication

- Patient education materials

- Consent forms

Limited health literacy increases the chances that your patient will not understand her condition, your recommended treatment, and treatment alternatives. She may also have a hard time complying with your instructions for self-care and follow-up. All these increase the risk of a poor outcome and potentially a related medical professional liability claim. To assist patients with suspected limited health literacy, you can:

- Find out whether your patient understands what you have told her and any written materials you provided. Certain groups of patients are more likely to have low health literacy, but you should not assume that others do not. The only way to know if your patient understands is to ask her.

- If you use standard patient education materials, make sure the reading level is appropriate to the individual patient.

- A patient may be reluctant to tell you she cannot read or reads poorly. Asking whether any written materials you provided were helpful might encourage her to tell you if she could not read or fully understand them.

A patient may appear to be noncompliant, miss appointments, or not follow up on referrals for consultations or tests. Consider health literacy problems as an explanation.

Communicating Via E-mail

Many of your patients may have access to the Internet and e-mail accounts. E-mail offers opportunities for improving communication with your patients. Possible benefits of using e-mail include:

- Avoiding telephone tag

- Providing written information for the patient's future reference

- Providing a written record of the physician–patient communication

E-mail communication also raises issues related to privacy, confidentiality, security, and medical professional liability risk. For example, you could accidentally send a patient's e-mail to someone else, or an unauthorized person could access patients' e-mail messages. The next few paragraphs will highlight these issues, make suggestions for developing your practice's e-mail policies and procedures, and point you to additional resources.

If you want to enhance communication with your patients by using e-mail, it is advisable to develop policies and procedures specifically for e-mail. Issues you will want to discuss and consider include the following:

- What types of communication with patients do you want to take place through e-mail? Appointment scheduling and other administrative tasks? Prescription refill requests? Medical advice? Test results?

- What types of communication should *not* be handled by e-mail? Are there topics you do not want to discuss with patients through e-mail? For example, you might decide that prenatal genetic testing results will not be conveyed through e-mail.

- How often will you be able to check e-mail? What will your turnaround time be for responding?

- Will nonphysician staff review and triage e-mail messages?

- How will you protect the privacy and security of patient e-mail communications?

- How will you ensure that e-mail communications with a patient are incorporated into her medical record?

When you have determined your e-mail policies and procedures, you should put them in writing and make sure office staff have been informed of, trained on, and adhere to your e-mail policies. Also add the e-mail policies and procedures to your office's Notice of Privacy Practices (see Chapter 12). Following are a few key suggestions for ensuring that incorporating e-mail into your patient communications does not expose you to greater liability risk:

- Develop procedures to ensure that e-mail messages do not fall through the cracks.

- Be sure patients understand your e-mail policies and procedures. If a patient wants to communicate by e-mail, you may want to have her read and sign a copy of your practice's e-mail policy. Keep a copy in her medical record.

- Stress to patients that they should not use e-mail for urgent problems or emergencies. If staff will be handling patient e-mails, develop guidelines for handling messages that require prompt action or immediate referral to a physician.

- Limit e-mail communications to patients with whom you have already established a physician–patient relationship.

E-mail is certainly faster than regular mail. The ability to respond to a patient or a colleague when you are available, instead of exchanging multiple telephone calls, is clearly convenient for the typical busy ob-gyn. However, the speed with which you can send e-mail and the lack of direct contact could lead to errors and misunderstandings. To reduce the chances of miscommunication, take the following precautions when sending e-mail:

- Use as much care in composing an e-mail to a patient or colleague as you would in writing or dictating a letter.

- Pay close attention to the tone of your e-mail. Do not be sarcastic or attempt humor.

- Remember that the nonverbal communication (eg, facial expressions, body language) that helps convey meaning in face-to-face conversations will be absent from e-mail.

- Always proofread e-mail before you send it. Misspellings and grammatical errors give the impression that you are a sloppy physician. Errors could provide incorrect information.

The American Medical Association has developed e-mail guidelines that address communication issues, medical–legal issues, and ethics of e-mail communication with patients. These guidelines, along with guidelines from the American Medical Informatics Association (www.amia.org), may be helpful in developing your practice's e-mail policies.

Giving Bad News: Disclosing Adverse Outcomes and Medical Errors

Regardless of your skills as an ob-gyn, it is almost certain that sometime one of your patients will experience an unanticipated poor outcome. Effective and sensitive communication skills are never more important than when you must deliver bad news. Whether you are telling a patient and her family that a complication arising from a known risk has occurred or you are disclosing a medical error, how you handle the conversation could affect whether the patient files a claim, as well as the outcome of that claim.

The patient safety movement and patient advocates urge physicians to tell patients promptly about adverse outcomes and errors and, if appropriate, apologize. They argue that:

- Patients have a right to know about everything that has happened to them. This information could influence decisions about future care.

- If a physician or institution has made a mistake, patients and their family members want to know what happened, receive an apology, and be assured that future mistakes will be prevented.

- Many medical liability claims result from the feeling of patients and family members that a physician or hospital tried to hide information.

- Disclosing an error right away might prevent a lengthy medical professional liability case that could be stressful and painful for everyone concerned. If providing compensation would be appropriate, settlement discussions could proceed quickly.

A number of factors support the push for disclosure of errors and adverse outcomes:

- As a physician, you have an ethical obligation to be truthful and honest with patients.

- Your hospital must meet requirements by the Joint Commission (formerly the Joint Commission on Accreditation of Healthcare Organizations [JCAHO]) to implement processes to disclose unanticipated outcomes to patients and families.

- Some institutions that have implemented early disclosure policies report positive experiences and an actual reduction in the amount of liability claims paid.

However, the not unreasonable fear of being sued and having your own words used against you in court can serve as a powerful deterrent to an open discussion about a poor outcome or mistake with a patient and her family. This publication cannot provide a detailed discussion of the pros and cons of disclosing errors or apologizing to patients. The following suggestions can help you begin thinking about how you will handle this issue in your practice:

- Learn about the legal climate in your state affecting physicians' disclosure and apology. Your state medical society or local medical liability defense attorneys may be good sources of information.

- Be sure you understand any requirements under your medical liability insurance policy for early notification of incidents (see Chapter 10, "Professional Liability Insurance").

- Become familiar with your hospital's policies and procedures for disclosing adverse outcomes and errors. The hospital risk management program may offer training and assistance.

- If your patient experiences a complication, unanticipated poor outcome, or an error, do not avoid her or her family. Lack of information and contact with you could lead to feelings of frustration and abandonment, as well as a sense that you are trying to hide something.

- When talking with the patient and her family about what has happened, stick to the facts. If you do not yet know how or why the incident occurred, say so and explain how you will go about obtaining and sharing the necessary information.

- Be prepared for the patient or family members to be angry and distressed.

- If there is a need for additional care, be sure to explain what is needed and how the care will be provided.

- Express sympathy and regret, if appropriate. Choose your words carefully.

If you have taken the steps discussed in this chapter to establish an open collaborative dialogue with your patient, the chances of a productive discussion

If your patient experiences a complication, unanticipated poor outcome, or an error, do not avoid her or her family.

about a poor outcome or a medical error will be greater than if you did not. There is no guarantee, though, that disclosing and apologizing for a medical error will protect you from being sued.

Terminating the Physician–Patient Relationship

You have an ethical and legal obligation to continue providing care to a patient with whom you have established a physician–patient relationship. This obligation, however, does not continue indefinitely. Under some circumstances you might find it necessary to terminate the physician–patient relationship. These circumstances could include:

- You are closing your practice because of relocation or retirement.

- A patient is noncompliant, disruptive, or abusive.

- A patient has not paid outstanding bills, in spite of your repeated attempts to address the nonpayment.

- You feel that you cannot meet a patient's unrealistic expectations for her care.

- You are changing the scope of your practice—for example, dropping obstetrics.

Although you do have the right to stop providing care to a patient in a number of situations, you must terminate the relationship properly. If you do not follow appropriate procedures for terminating a physician–patient relationship and a patient suffers harm, you could be vulnerable to charges of patient abandonment. A successful claim of patient abandonment must demonstrate the following:

- You terminated the physician–patient relationship at an unreasonable time.

- You failed to provide the patient with enough notice so that she could find another qualified physician.

- Your inappropriate termination of the relationship caused the patient's injury.

To terminate the physician–patient relationship properly, focus on ensuring continuity of care for the patient. The key elements are making reasonable attempts to provide both adequate notice of the termination and assistance in finding another source of care and documenting those efforts with care:

- Provide advance written notice of termination. The appropriate time period can vary. In some circumstances, 30 days is adequate notice, but some patients may need more time.

- Include in the written notice your reasons for withdrawing from the patient's care. Be sure you state the reasons objectively and have documentation that supports those reasons.

- Note the patient's current medical condition and her needs for ongoing care.

- Provide information to help her find another physician. You could include a list of other ob-gyns in the community or the telephone number of a medical society or hospital physician referral service.

- Offer to provide copies of medical records to the patient's new physician. You may want to include authorization for transferring records for the patient to complete when she finds a new physician.

- Retain a copy of the letter, and document that the patient received the letter. Registered mail with a return receipt is a good, though not required, procedure.

Obstetric patients require special consideration for terminating the physician–patient relationship:

- Pregnant patients might need more time to find another obstetrician.

- A patient in her third trimester may be unable to find another physician to care for her, so terminating the relationship might not be feasible or appropriate.

If you are closing your practice or discontinuing obstetric services, plan to continue providing care until delivery for patients who are already in the third trimester. Assist first- and second-trimester patients in finding another obstetrician.

There are some circumstances in which you cannot terminate a physician–patient relationship:

- Dismissing a patient based on race, religion, disability, ethnic origin, age, or, in some locations, sexual orientation can violate federal, state, or local laws and professional ethical standards.

- Your agreements with health plans might restrict your ability to end a physician–patient relationship with a plan member. Check your contracts carefully.

- Terminating the physician–patient relationship when the patient is unstable or in advanced pregnancy could leave you open to charges of patient abandonment.

Ending a physician–patient relationship requires the same honest, respectful communication skills you used to begin the relationship. Clear and sensitive communication, adequate notice, and careful documentation can help you avoid possible harm to the patient's health and an increase in your liability risk.

Working hard to communicate effectively with your patients is well worth the effort. If you take the time to listen to patients, explain what you are doing and why, and answer questions completely, you will probably find it easier to provide the kind of care you want to offer. You may be more satisfied with your work and patient interactions. And, as an added benefit, you could reduce your liability risk.

KEY POINTS

✓ Effective physician–patient communication is essential to good patient care.

✓ When an adverse outcome occurs, good communication skills may reduce the chance of litigation.

✓ Be aware of potential communication barriers—cultural and language differences, limited health literacy, disabilities—and work to overcome them.

✓ E-mail can be an effective communication tool, but policies and procedures need to be established to prevent e-mail from becoming a liability risk.

✓ If you must terminate a physician–patient relationship, be sure you follow the proper process to avoid charges of patient abandonment.

Chapter 8

Medical Records and Documentation

As a practicing ob-gyn or ob-gyn resident, you have undoubtedly seen firsthand how the quality of the information in a patient's chart can either make your job easier and enhance patient care or make your job much tougher. Although good documentation and medical record keeping do not guarantee good patient care, poor documentation may very well hinder good care. If you are in practice, you have seen that documentation practices also can affect your practice's financial performance.

Good medical record keeping reduces your exposure to medical professional liability claims by minimizing chances for miscommunication among the health care team. If you are sued, the patient's medical record can be your best ally or your worst enemy:

- Well documented, complete records can demonstrate that you met the standard of care.

- A complete, accurate chart will support your assertion that you are a careful, thorough physician.

- Poor records—illegible, skimpy, or altered—may suggest that your diagnosis and treatment were sloppy and that you are careless.

Poor documentation practices could force you to settle a claim that you could have easily defended, if you had documented the care you did provide.

This chapter will discuss major principles of medical record documentation:

- Accuracy

- Comprehensiveness

- Legibility

- Objectivity

- Timeliness

In addition, the proper way to correct medical records and special issues related to electronic medical records will be addressed.

Review your documentation practices with these principles in mind. You may find room for improvements that will make it easier to provide high-quality care, strengthen your coding and reimbursement, and reduce your liability risk. (For a

If you are sued, the patient's medical record can be your best ally or your worst enemy.

quick overview of record keeping and documentation issues, see Appendix E risk management checklist, "Medical Records and Documentation.")

Accuracy

The medical record is a major tool you use to communicate with other physicians and providers caring for your patients. Serious harm can occur if the information in the patient's chart is inaccurate or if others interpret your notes differently than you intended. Good practices include the following:

- Use your hospital's standard method for recording entries in the patient's hospital chart.

- If there is a special circumstance and you are a resident, ask for guidance from your residency program director.

- Be consistent in word use.

- Choose your words carefully, especially when there is a chance for confusion (eg, "extraction" or "delivery").

- Use only abbreviations that all providers involved have agreed on. For example, is SBE self breast examination or subacute bacterial endocarditis?

- Consider developing a list of approved abbreviations to be used in your practice. (Some hospitals have lists of acceptable abbreviations.)

- Note all events in the course of treatment with the time, date, and a legible signature.

Ordering medications and documenting prescriptions calls for several precautions:

- Beware of the "wayward decimal." Putting the decimal point in the wrong spot will cause a 10-fold difference in the dose—potentially a life or death mistake.

- Double-check dosage calculations based on patient weight.

- Be sure you have written the correct name of the drug clearly. Many drugs have similar names and can be confused easily.

Automated electronic physician order entry systems hold promise for reducing medication errors. You should support initiatives for introducing such systems in your hospital and office.

Comprehensiveness

Look at one of your patients' medical records. If you did not know this patient and had to take over her care, would her record tell you everything you needed to know? A comprehensive medical record provides all clinically pertinent information about the patient, including:

- Details of her current condition

- Past medical and surgical history

- Relevant family and social history
- Results of physical examinations, laboratory tests, diagnostic procedures, and risk identification and screening tools
- Operative reports and procedure notes
- Consultant reports
- Documentation of informed consent discussions
- All patient correspondence
- Complete documentation of care during labor and delivery
    —Always dictate a delivery note for complicated or operative deliveries (eg, forceps and vacuum, shoulder dystocia).
    —Consider dictating a brief note for every delivery.

Electronic fetal heart rate monitoring strips can be especially problematic. Inconsistent use of terminology to describe fetal heart rate tracings could jeopardize patient safety and increase your liability risk. It is essential that everyone caring for the patient in labor have a common understanding of what the electronic fetal monitor strip means:

- Ensure that all members of the labor and delivery team are speaking the same language in interpreting and documenting fetal heart rate patterns.
- Use the current standard nomenclature for electronic fetal monitoring used by the 1997 National Institute of Child Health and Human Development (NICHD). (It is anticipated that the NICHD will convene a consensus conference on electronic fetal monitoring nomenclature in 2008 with the specific objective of recommending standard nomenclature.)
- Keep any electronic fetal monitoring strips, tracings, and notes with the patient's record.

Using the nomenclature used by the NICHD will help to improve the quality of care your patients receive by reducing the chances for miscommunication. If you are sued, your use of the accepted terminology will enhance your defense, especially if the plaintiff's expert uses nonstandard terminology.

Check to see if someone else reviewing your documentation of the diagnostic workup and treatment plan could easily understand:

- The information you evaluated (eg, history, physical examination findings, laboratory results)
- The alternatives you considered—including significant competing diagnoses you ruled out
- The treatment you recommended
- Your reasoning and rationale for arriving at a diagnosis
- Your reasons for choosing the treatment

- If applicable, your reason(s) for deviating from the most commonly accepted mode of care, practice guideline, or treatment algorithm
- If applicable, your reason(s) for not following a consultant's recommendations

The medical record also should reflect the patient's response to your treatment recommendations, including:

- Her informed consent to your treatment plan, including topics covered during the informed consent discussion
- Compliance or noncompliance with your recommended treatment plan
- Failure to keep appointments and your attempts to follow-up
- Questions, concerns, and comments—both positive and negative—on the treatment and her progress
- Informed refusal of recommended diagnostic or treatment services

You probably have a substantial amount of contact with patients other than in-person visits. Telephone conversations frequently play a key role in medical professional liability claims. Your written notes of a telephone conversation will be more convincing than a recollection long after the call occurred. Include the following information in the patient's record:

- Copies of all telephone messages.
- Detailed notes of all telephone conversations
- Copies of all patient e-mails (see Chapter 7, "Patient Communication," for a discussion of e-mail communication with patients).

Nursing notes are a critical part of the medical record, especially for hospitalized patients:

- Read all nursing notes carefully.
- Correct or augment the nursing notes as needed (see this chapter's section, "Correcting Medical Records").
- Examine nursing notes on electronic fetal monitoring strips with particular care.

Let this canard of the plaintiff's attorney be your guide for how much to record: "If it is not documented, it did not happen!"

Legibility

The medical record is your voice when you are not present to take care of your patient. The other physicians, nurses, and health providers you trust to help care for your patients must be able to understand what you say:

- Do not make your colleagues waste valuable time or cause them to misunderstand the patient's status or the care you provided because they cannot read what you wrote.

- Do not allow a plaintiff's attorney or a jury to conclude that you provided sloppy care or no care at all because your notes are sloppy and illegible.

- Take the time you need to write legibly and neatly.

Objectivity

Far too many medical professional liability claims result from inappropriate, nonfactual remarks physicians make or record in a patient's chart. If you do not want to be the victim of a colleague's unprofessional observations in a medical record, do your part to set the right example:

- Confine remarks in a medical record to facts and legitimate, objective clinical judgments.

- Do not use the medical record to criticize a colleague's care of the patient.

- Do not use the patient's chart as a vehicle for resolving differences of opinion about diagnosis or treatment. If you have questions or concerns, bring them up directly with your colleagues.

- Avoid using vague, subjective, or judgmental words. Be specific and factual.

- Do not make unnecessary, irrelevant comments about a patient's ethnicity or other personal characteristics. Ask yourself, is this comment important for the patient's care?

Do not use the patient's chart as a vehicle for resolving differences of opinion about diagnosis or treatment. If you have questions or concerns, bring them up directly with your colleagues.

Timeliness

Everyone involved in a patient's care should be kept up-to-date on her condition, the treatment she has received, and any new findings. Timely information is necessary for providing appropriate care. If the patient's care becomes the subject of a medical professional liability claim, the sequence of events—what you knew and when you knew it—could be crucial to your defense. Follow these guidelines for timeliness:

- Record all events or facts when they occur or when you learn about them.

- Do not delay; a lapse of time increases the chances that another provider will not have the information she or he needs or that you will not remember correctly or completely.

- Review, interpret, and sign or initial all laboratory and other diagnostic test results in a timely fashion.

- Set up a method for ensuring that you review, act on, and record all test results (see Chapter 5, "Risk Management").

Correcting Medical Records

A bedrock principle of medical record documentation you probably learned as a medical student is that the medical record must never be altered. Although it is true that you should never remove or obscure information in a patient's record, you will find times when it is necessary to correct an error. Be sure you make the correction properly:

- If you are a resident, first notify the attending physician that the record needs to be corrected.

- Place the new entry below the last entry in the chart.

- Explain the need for the change and include the time, date, and your signature or initials.

- Draw a single line through the incorrect entry, making sure it is still readable.

- Do not scratch out, white out, or write over the incorrect entry.

- Do not insert new information into an entry you or someone else made previously.

- Do not try to squeeze corrections into margins or at the bottom of a page.

Make necessary corrections to medical records as soon as you realize that you made an error in documentation. Never make changes to a medical record after a claim has been filed or after an incident occurs that is likely to result in a claim. If another physician has made an error, bring it to his or her attention as soon as possible and take necessary steps to make sure that no other providers act on the incorrect information.

Using the proper method to make any corrections will make it clear that you were ensuring the completeness and accuracy of the record. Changing the medical record improperly could be damaging to your defense of a medical liability claim:

- Inconsistent, damaged, or altered records or records with entries removed or obscured suggest that you are trying to hide something.

- A jury may not see you as a credible witness if there is evidence you tampered with the medical record.

- An impression that you changed the medical record improperly could make it hard to defend the case and increase the size of an award.

- You could be charged with perjury if you claim under oath that the record was unaltered if you did change it.

The Health Insurance Portability and Accountability Act (HIPAA) gives patients the right to examine their medical records and request corrections. If a patient requests that you make a correction to her record and you decide that the correction is appropriate (you do have the right to refuse to make the change), follow the principles outlined above to implement the correction. (See Chapter 12, "Government Requirements Affecting Medical Practice," for more information about HIPAA.)

Electronic Medical Records

Computerized electronic medical record (EMR) systems can help you improve the quality of your medical record keeping. Once you invest the time to learn the system documentation will be less burdensome. Advantages of an EMR include the following:

- Entries are legible.

- All entries have date and time included.

- E-mail messages can be included automatically in the record.

- Telephone messages and notes from calls can be included.

- Some systems allow remote access, for example, from your home when you are on call.

- Some systems provide clinical decision support tools or reminders. For example, the system might prompt you to order a mammogram for a 50-year-old patient who is in the office for her annual well-woman visit.

- Some systems allow you to write standardized text for frequently encountered situations. For example, you could input a standard description of your typical well-woman examination.

Along with their promise for improving the process of medical record keeping, EMRs bring some special medical professional liability concerns. If you use an EMR system:

- Become familiar with HIPAA requirements for security of electronically stored patient information (see Chapter 12).

- Establish appropriate limits on who has access to records and the ability to alter or make entries.

- Ensure that staff is properly trained in the use of the EMR system.

- Document your reasons for not following the system's decision support tools or prompts.

- Customize standardized text as needed for each patient.

Investing the time needed to place legible, complete entries in a patient's chart can seem like an unreasonable burden when your day is filled with hospital rounds, surgery or deliveries, and a busy office. The time you save today by skimping on your documentation could be spent tomorrow trying to remember the details or deciphering your own hurried handwriting. Failure to document completely the good care you provided could cost you time and much more in a medical liability claim.

KEY POINTS

✓ Good documentation does not guarantee good patient care, but poor documentation can hinder it.

✓ If you are sued, thorough, legible records will aid your defense.

✓ Poor record keeping could force you to settle an otherwise defensible claim.

✓ All entries in the medical record should be complete, legible, objective, and timely.

✓ Make only factual, relevant entries in the medical record. Do not use the patient's chart to question another physician's care.

✓ Follow the proper procedure for correcting errors in the medical record.

Chapter 9

Special Liability Issues for Residents

If you are an ob-gyn resident, you should become familiar with all the topics included in this book. Knowledge of these medical professional liability issues will be important to you during your residency and in your future practice. In addition, there are a number of medical liability issues specific to residency that you should be aware of throughout your training. If you have completed residency, but work with residents in any capacity, it is important for you to understand residents' special medical liability status and how it may affect you. This chapter will focus on:

- Residents' medical professional liability status
- Being sued during residency
- Ethical issues for residents
- Medical professional liability issues for supervisory physicians

Residents' Medical Professional Liability Status

As a resident in training, you work under some degree of supervision at all times, even if you are a fully licensed physician. Supervisors can include full-time attending physicians, part-time or volunteer clinical faculty and community physicians, senior residents, residency program director, and other hospital staff. Your dual role as a physician caring for patients and a trainee working under supervision creates medical professional liability issues unique to residency:

- You can be held legally responsible for your actions. (More than 37% of ob-gyns responding to the 2006 ACOG Survey on Professional Liability had been sued for an incident that happened during residency.)
- Physicians supervising you can be held accountable for what you do.

A medical liability claim against you could result from a patient not knowing or misunderstanding your status as a resident. The following points are important:

- Make sure your name badge identifying you as a resident is clearly visible.
- Always explain to patients that you are a resident working under the supervision of another physician. Be sure the patient understands that another physician will be involved in her care.

Even though you are still in training, a court is likely to hold you to the same standard of care as a fully trained, board-certified ob-gyn.

- Respect a patient's wishes if she does not want to have residents involved in her care.

It may be unlikely that a patient will file a claim simply because she did not know you were a resident. However, if she is dissatisfied with her care or has an adverse outcome, your failure to disclose your residency status could contribute to her decision to file a medical liability claim.

Usually a resident is named in claims asserting that she or he did not meet the appropriate standard of care. Even though you are still in training, a court is likely to hold you to the same standard of care as a fully trained, board-certified ob-gyn. Do not put yourself and your patients at unnecessary risk:

- Remember that you do not have the skills and expertise of a fully trained ob-gyn.

- Provide only services you have been trained for and are authorized to perform. Performing procedures that go beyond your qualifications puts you in a very weak position if you are sued.

- Do not attempt to handle everything alone. Even the most skilled and experienced physician cannot handle all patient care challenges alone.

Communicating well with supervising physicians is key to providing appropriate care and making sure you practice within the scope of your training. Your responsibilitites include the following:

- Let the supervising physician know when the patient needs care you cannot provide.

- Learn the proper way to transfer ("handoff") patient care and continue to refine this skill.

- Ensure that the attending physician is aware of the scope and urgency of the patient's needs.

- Keep the patient and her family informed about what is happening. Make sure she is comfortable with the care you are providing and let her know that the attending physician is also available to her.

In the best of all possible worlds, a resident would never be placed in the position of questioning the judgment of an attending physician. If this does happen, however, keep these points in mind:

- The attending physician might have information about the patient that you do not know, for example, details of her history, physical examination, laboratory tests, or imaging studies.

- The patient may have asked the attending physician to keep some information confidential.

- If the situation were to become an issue in a medical liability claim, the jury is unlikely to believe that you had more knowledge and greater expertise than the attending physician.

- The accepted standard of care might include alternative diagnostic and treatment approaches of which you are unaware.

Only the attending physician has the ultimate authority to direct treatment. Attending physicians teach and supervise residents. Roles rarely are reversed. If you have authority to treat the patient, it is because the attending physician has delegated that authority to you. He or she remains vicariously liable for your acts or omissions.

Instances in which a resident has a compelling claim to exercise authority over an attending physician are rare. Such cases almost always are limited to allegedly wanton or willful acts of negligence by an attending physician, usually gross negligence, which would be inherently harmful to a patient. In the unlikely event that an attending physician's action or inaction puts a patient at risk of harm, you should:

- First and foremost, tell the attending physician immediately and directly about your concerns and questions. Ask him or her to explain what is being done or not done. Have this conversation in private and be respectful.

- If you remain concerned after a discussion with the attending physician, try to communicate immediately with the supervisory attending physician of the day, the clinical chief of service, or the residency program director to clarify the patient care plan.

- Continue to visit the patient on rounds and perform all assigned duties, including the writing of progress notes, if you have been assigned to do so. Record the patient's subjective comments and complaints, as well as all objective findings, including laboratory test results and results of other diagnostic and imaging modalities.

- Limit your notes in the patient's chart to observations of fact. Omit the "assessment" and "plan" portions of recorded progress notes in the hospital record until your questions about the treatment plan have been clarified.

- Do not use the patient record to document your disagreement with the attending physician's care.

- If you feel that it is in your interest to maintain your own record of the patient's care, including your assessment of the patient's condition and recommended plan of treatment, you may do so.

- Remember that any private notes or records will be discoverable in the event of litigation. Again, such notes should reflect only facts, not suppositions or judgments, and should not express medically unfounded opinion.

Being Sued During Residency

You could be named in a medical professional liability claim during your residency. An allegation of medical negligence is extremely distressing for any physician. If you are a resident, you may be especially ill-prepared to cope with the stress generated by a medical liability claim:

- You do not have years of successful practice to draw upon to bolster your confidence. The self-doubt that plagues many physicians who have been sued might be even greater for you, a physician still in training.

- You might be concerned about your status in the residency program and the possibility of losing the regard of attending physicians and fellow residents.

- You might not know where to begin in responding to the claim.

Recognizing that the possibility of being named in a medical liability lawsuit is real and taking steps to learn what to do may help you manage better if you are sued. You can also prepare yourself to help if one of your fellow residents is sued.

A detailed introduction to the civil litigation process is provided in Appendix A, "What To Do If You Are Sued." Review that appendix with care. A number of points made in the appendix bear repeating here. In addition, as a resident, you may have some unique concerns about being sued. This section will discuss:

- Your first response to the claim

- Communicating with supervising physicians and peers about the case

- Getting the support you need

Your First Response to the Claim

Receiving a summons and complaint can be a traumatic event, especially if it is served in a public setting, which still happens in some states. Regardless of how upset you may be, you cannot afford to delay responding:

- The mechanics of civil litigation require that an "Answer to the Complaint" be served immediately—within 10–30 days in most jurisdictions.

- If your Answer to a Summons and Complaint is not timely, a summary judgment could be entered against you. That is, you would lose the case without a chance to defend yourself.

If you were a practicing physician, you would immediately notify your medical professional liability insurance carrier. As a resident, though, your residency program provides your insurance, so you must work through the institution's procedures for responding to a medical liability claim. Do not wait until you have been named in lawsuit to find out what your program's procedures are. Make it your job to find out now whom you should notify and to whom you must deliver the Summons and Complaint. The process will vary among different residency programs:

- In some programs, the hospital's or medical school's risk management department or legal affairs office is designated to receive and respond to the documents.

- In some programs, the program director or department chair's office is the first point of contact.

Promptly take the following actions if you are named in a lawsuit:

- Notify your program director.

- Deliver the Summons and Complaint to the designated person or office immediately.

- Obtain a receipt or a signed and dated note.

- Obtain a copy of the documents.

An attorney will be assigned to defend you. It is essential to cooperate fully with your attorney. (See Appendix A and Chapter 10, "Professional Liability Insurance," for a discussion of working effectively with your attorney.) Information you provide to your attorney is protected by attorney–client privilege and cannot be used as evidence. However, your attorney will be inclined to focus on the facts of the case and is not likely to be able to serve as your main source of emotional support.

Sometimes perceived or potentially real conflicts of interest arise between a resident and his or her assigned defense attorney. You should notify your program director if:

- You feel unable to work effectively with the assigned defense attorney.

- You feel that a conflict of interest exists because your assigned attorney represents other defendants whose interests may be in opposition to your own.

Your program director will assist you in determining whether another attorney should and can be assigned.

Communicating With Supervisors and Peers About the Case

One of the first things your attorney may tell you is not to discuss the case with anyone else. This is an important caution. Most physicians have a strong sense of responsibility for others and may tend to be self-critical. These tendencies might lead you to express remorse about what happened to the patient and doubt about the care you provided during discussions with your colleagues. In addition, as a resident you are accustomed to discussing and reviewing the care you provide with attending physicians and resident peers in your continuing efforts to learn and improve your skills. Such discussion could be detrimental to your case:

- Conversations like these are not protected communications and could be used as evidence in court.

- A lay jury unfamiliar with the culture of medicine might interpret your efforts to learn and improve patient care as admissions of error.

Supervising physicians, your program director, and your fellow residents should, and most likely will, understand and respect your need to avoid discussing the clinical and legal details of the case. After all, they also are ob-gyns who are vulnerable to medical liability lawsuits.

Residents always work under the supervision of another physician. Therefore, it is likely that an attending physician—either a full-time faculty

You probably will feel a strong need to talk about your emotions and the lawsuit's impact.

member or a private attending physician—will be a codefendant in the lawsuit against you. A codefendant physician might want to discuss the case to find out whether you are "on his or her side." For the most part, such conversations should take place with your respective attorneys present to protect both physicians. On the other hand, it is not unreasonable or inappropriate to confirm facts, verify chart entries, and maintain a cordial professional relationship with the attending physician involved. You should not, however, participate in any effort to coordinate or influence testimony or alter the medical record.

Getting the Support You Need

Avoiding any and all discussions about the case will be difficult and is probably unwise for your mental health. You probably will feel a strong need to talk about your emotions and the lawsuit's impact. Also, you probably will want emotional and professional support from your colleagues and supervisors in your residency program. To get the help you need without jeopardizing your defense, ideally, your residency program and sponsoring institution would have a broad array of both practical and emotional support services. These could include:

- Leniency about taking time off to prepare for your case

- Medical professional liability coverage that pays for the services of a mental health professional specializing in support for defendant physicians

- Health benefits that provide generous coverage of mental health services

- An employee assistance program to help employees cope with stressful life events

In real life, though, resources available to residency programs vary greatly and may, in fact, be very limited. Supervising physicians and resident peers may hesitate to provide the emotional support that you need and they would like to provide because they fear—with good cause—that talking with you about the case could complicate your defense. As a result, you may need to find your own sources of help.

Your spouse, family members, and close friends are a natural source of support. In addition, the lawsuit is probably a traumatic event for them as well. Although you cannot discuss the legal or clinical details of the case, you can seek and provide emotional support by talking about some aspects of the situation:

- The lawsuit is public, so you can disclose the fact that you have been sued.

- The allegations in the case are also public, so you can provide a basic explanation of what the case is about without discussing the medical facts or patient care.

- If you are confident that you did everything you could and provided appropriate care, you can say so.

- You can talk about how you feel and how the case affects you, as long as you do not talk about the details of the care you provided.

- You might also decide to seek professional help. In general,

    —Communications with a psychiatrist or other physician who is treating you are protected from discovery.

    —Discussion with a nonphysician mental health professional usually is protected from disclosure.

    —Conversations with clergy–therapists are usually protected from disclosure as well.

State laws vary. Talk with your attorney about whether the court will recognize conversations with your selected mental health professional as confidential.

Many physicians, even the most skilled and experienced, are sued for medical liability. Few ob-gyns will escape a lawsuit. Nearly all physicians who are sued find that it is among the most stressful experiences of their lives. Chapter 11, "Coping With the Stress of a Medical Professional Liability Claim," provides a detailed discussion about coping with the stress of professional liability litigation. Remember that help is available. Be sure to get the help you need so you can continue to function successfully and complete your training.

Ethical Issues for Residents

As a resident, you have little choice about the patients you see, the procedures you perform, and the physicians with whom you work. You may face situations that challenge your own ethical, moral, or religious principles. The following actions will help you handle these situations:

- The best time to find out the procedures you should follow and resources available to you to resolve dilemmas like these is before the situation arises.

- Learn your residency program's protocols for services that you find objectionable for whatever reason.

- Find out whether the hospital or residency program has specific procedures or resources to help you address ethical dilemmas.

- Obtain and review copies of the department policies and hospital procedures.

- Know the chain of command for reporting problems. Should you first discuss problems with your chief resident, then the program director? If not, what is the appropriate procedure?

- Talk with more senior residents and attending physicians about possible informal ways for addressing ethical dilemmas.

Care You Are Not Trained to Provide

Always be aware of the limitations of your own skills, knowledge, and expertise. Remember, too, that not every supervising physician will be familiar with the details and extent of your training and abilities. If asked to perform a duty beyond your training, follow these guidelines:

- When you work without direct supervision, perform only procedures for which you have been fully trained.

- Do not provide a service you are not qualified to perform. Ask for assistance.

- Follow your program's procedures for requesting help or refusing to provide a service.

- If there is no specific protocol, make your request through the hospital's chain of command.

If no one is available to substitute for you or assist you, you will have to weigh the risks. Is the risk of harm greater if you provide the service or will the patient suffer more harm if you do not provide care? The following points are important:

- Always let the patient's best interest and your best judgment guide you.

- If not providing care is likely to cause greater harm, provide the necessary care to the best of your ability.

- Be sure to document your efforts to find someone more qualified to take over or assist you.

Care You Oppose

Ob-gyn care not infrequently involves services some physicians might object to on moral, ethical, or religious grounds (eg, abortion, sterilization, in vitro fertilization). Every physician tries to practice in a way that is consistent with her or his personal beliefs. As a resident, though, you might feel unsure about how you can appropriately reconcile residency requirements with your ethical or religious principles. If you object to certain types of procedures, express your concerns:

- Let your program director know as soon as you can. Early notification gives the program director and supervising physicians time to plan ahead.

- Avoid waiting to make your objections known until you are asked to participate in a procedure you oppose.

The Accreditation Council for Graduate Medical Education requirements mandate that residency programs allow residents who object to abortion to decline to participate in abortion training; ACOG policy supports this mandate.

If you decline to perform a procedure because of personal, moral, or ethical objections, you can still counsel patients, make referrals to other sources of care, and manage complications.

Working With an Impaired or Incompetent Physician

You may find yourself working with or under the supervision of an impaired or incompetent physician. In this situation, it is appropriate that you:

- Give the patient's welfare your first priority.

- Ask more senior residents, supervising physicians, or your program director for guidance.

- Follow any hospital protocols for encouraging impaired physicians to get help.

- If there are no specific procedures in place, follow the institution's usual chain of command for reporting problems.

If you encounter an emergency situation in which no one is available to provide guidance or take over for the impaired physician, take the following steps:

- If the patient is at risk of immediate harm, intervene to protect her.

- Ask senior hospital staff for help as soon as possible.

- Document your actions and the reasons you took the steps you did.

Medical Professional Liability Issues for Supervisory Physicians

If you supervise residents, you should be aware that you can be held liable for a resident's actions through vicarious liability. If a resident is working under your supervision, he or she is considered your agent and you are responsible for what he or she does or fails to do. Several legal doctrines may affect supervising physicians:

- *Respondeat superior* or "let the master speak"—a supervisor is responsible for the actions of someone he supervises

- *Borrowed servant*—you can be held liable for the actions of someone else's employee (eg, a resident employed by the hospital) if that employee was uniquely appropriated to work under your direction

- *Captain-of-the-ship*—you are responsible for the actions of those under your control and direction if you are in charge (eg, the surgical team, if you are the primary surgeon)

It is important to recognize that even if you are not an employee of the residency program or hospital, you might still be held responsible for the actions of residents you supervise under the borrowed servant or captain-of-the-ship doctrines. Application of these doctrines varies from state to state. Consult with a local attorney to understand the interpretation in your state.

Although you as a supervising physician can be held responsible for a resident's actions, the hospital and residency program are liable as well. The hospital is liable for the negligent acts or omissions of a resident because the resident is a hospital employee. This liability applies if the negligent acts or omissions are within the scope of the resident's assigned duties and within the scope of the resident's training and experience.

Realize that you can be held liable for care provided by a resident you are supervising even when your involvement with the patient is very limited. A court could construe your assumption of supervisory responsibilities as establishing a physician–patient relationship with a resident's patients and a duty to provide them with reasonable care. For example, in *Mozingo v. Pitt County Memorial Hospital* 415 S.E. 2d 341 (N.C. 1992), the Supreme Court of North Carolina held a supervising ob-gyn liable for a resident's care even though he had never seen the patient:

- The ob-gyn had been taking call at home for several hours when a resident requested help managing a case of shoulder dystocia. The ob-gyn arrived after the baby was delivered with injuries.

- The ob-gyn asserted that he did not owe a duty of care to the patient and he provided supervision within the standard common in the state. He was dismissed from the case.

- The patient appealed and the Supreme Court of North Carolina found that the supervising ob-gyn did owe a duty of care to the patient being cared for by the residents he was supervising even though he had no prior contact with the patient.

Be aware of potential liability risks when agreeing to supervise residents. Consider vicarious liability issues when deciding how you will carry out your supervisory duties. Make sure you have a medical liability insurance policy that will cover you for claims related to supervising residents. If you supervise residents in a "moonlighting" activity, be aware that the medical liability insurance protection a resident receives from his or her residency program probably does not cover the moonlighting job.

KEY POINTS

If you are a resident...

✓ Although you always work under supervision, you can be held liable for the care you provide.

✓ In many cases you could be held to the same standard of care as a fully trained ob-gyn.

✓ Protect your patients and yourself. Never perform a procedure without direct supervision if you have not been trained.

✓ Identify resources to help you resolve ethical dilemmas that arise during residency.

If you work with residents...

✓ You are liable for the actions of the residents you supervise, even if you are a community physician not employed by the residency program.

✓ Become familiar with the interpretation of vicarious liability and related legal doctrines in your state.

✓ Make sure you have medical professional liability insurance coverage for your activities supervising residents.

Chapter 10

Professional Liability Insurance

Protection against the costs of being sued for medical professional liability is a necessity for both practicing ob-gyns and ob-gyn residents. Obstetrician–gynecologists responding to the 2006 ACOG Survey on Professional Liability reported being sued an average of 2.6 times in their medical careers. High damage awards are not uncommon. Although most cases do not result in a payment to the patient, legal costs can be significant.

Ensuring financial security for yourself, your family, and your practice most likely will require the purchase of medical liability insurance. The goal of this chapter is to help you become an educated consumer, able to select and retain the most appropriate coverage for your situation. Major topics covered include:

- Medical professional liability insurance basics (coverage, carriers, premiums, exclusions, and settlement options)

- Working effectively with your insurer

- Protecting your assets

- Coping with a crisis in your medical professional liability coverage

- Special medical professional liability issues for residents

Medical Professional Liability Insurance Basics

The world of insurance may be unfamiliar for many ob-gyns. To select the policy that is best for you and to understand what you have purchased, you will need to learn the language and basic operating principles of medical professional liability insurance. After reading this section you will understand:

- Key differences between occurrence and claims-made coverage

- What "tail" and "nose" coverages are and why they are important

- Limits of your coverage

- Sources of medical professional liability insurance coverage

- Common exclusions from coverage

- Options for settlement under your policy

Ob-gyns responding to the 2006 ACOG Survey on Professional Liability reported being sued an average of 2.6 times in their medical careers.

Occurrence, Claims-made, and Claims-paid Coverage: What's the Difference, and Why Does It Matter?

You may have heard the terms occurrence, claims-made, and claims-paid in reference to medical professional liability insurance. Understanding the fundamental differences among these types of medical liability insurance coverage is critical to feeling confident that you know what product you are buying.

Occurrence coverage covers you for all claims related to events that happen during the time the policy is in effect, regardless of when the claim is filed. This means that if you purchase an occurrence policy, the insurer issuing that policy will cover a claim for an incident that happened while you had that coverage even if you no longer are covered by that insurer:

- Occurrence policies are desirable for ob-gyns because claims for impaired infants may be made years after the events happened.

- Premiums may be more expensive than for other types of policies because of the coverage for future claims.

- Policy limits in force for your current policy will be those in effect for any future claims.

- An occurrence policy does not cover claims for incidents that happened before the policy was in effect, even if the claims are filed during the policy period.

- Many insurers have stopped issuing occurrence policies, so availability may be limited.

Claims-made coverage covers you for claims that are reported during the period the policy is in effect and that stem from an incident that occurred when the policy was in effect. In other words, both the incident stimulating the claim and the filing of the claim must happen while the policy is in effect, although not necessarily in the same policy year:

- A claims-made policy will not cover claims filed after the policy is no longer in effect, even though the incident occurred while the policy was in effect.

- Initially, premiums may be less expensive than for occurrence coverage.

- A claims-made policy does not cover claims for incidents that happened before the policy was in effect, even if the claim is filed during the policy period.

Claims-paid coverage covers you for claims in which all events related to the claim take place during the same policy year. This means that the incident must occur, the claim must be filed, the insurer notified, and any damages paid between the time you pay the premium for one year and the time the premium is due for the next year. Claims-paid coverage is relatively uncommon in ob-gyn practice:

- A claims-paid policy does not cover you if any of the key events do not take place within the policy year.

- Premiums are based on what the insurer expects to pay in claims during the policy year and typically are cheaper than other types of policies.

- If the insurer underestimates claims, policyholders usually will be required to pay an additional assessment to cover the losses.

- Patients often do not file claims immediately after an incident, and the legal system can move slowly, reducing the chances that all necessary events from incident to claim payment could occur within the policy year.

- An ob-gyn with claims-paid coverage might feel under strong pressure to settle a case quickly in order to have the claim paid.

If tail coverage is not affordable and available, you may find that future options for changing liability insurers or jobs are very limited.

"Tail Coverage" and "Nose Coverage": What Is It and Who Needs It?

One of the most important things to understand about a claims-made or claims-paid medical professional liability insurance policy is that when you leave the insurer that issued that policy, you are not covered for any future claims. It is absolutely essential to purchase either a reporting endorsement policy ("tail coverage") from your current insurer or a prior-acts policy ("nose coverage") from the subsequent insurer. What do these terms mean?

A reporting endorsement policy *("tail coverage")* covers you if a claim related to an incident that happened while you were insured under a claims-made policy is filed after that policy is no longer in effect:

- You must purchase the tail coverage from the insurer that issued the claims-made policy when it expires or you will not be covered for future claims.

- Cost of tail coverage may be from 2 to 10 times the amount of the last annual premium, depending on your number of years in practice and your claims experience.

Your coverage limits under the tail policy will usually be the same as under the claims-made policy. However, insurers apply these limits in various ways:

- Some renew the limits annually until after your death and probate of your estate.

- Some renew limits annually for several years after the coverage is purchased.

- Some apply the limits to the entire period the tail coverage is in effect. For example, a tail policy with "$1 million/$3 million limits" would pay up to $1 million per claim, but only a total of $3 million throughout the entire time the policy is in effect.

Be sure you understand how the limits of your tail coverage will work when you purchase the policy.

The provisions of available tail coverage may be spelled out in the claims-made policy you purchase, so you should make sure to understand these details fully when making your decision. If tail coverage is not affordable and available, you may find that future options for changing insurers or jobs are very limited.

A prior–acts policy *("nose coverage")* is an alternative to tail coverage. It is sometimes available from the liability carrier from whom you are purchasing your next claims-made policy. If you are not able or choose not to purchase tail coverage from the insurer you are leaving, a prior-acts policy provides coverage for claims filed after your previous claims-made policy has expired (for incidents occurring while it was in effect).

Understanding Policy Limits: How Much Insurance Do You Need?

Before determining the amount of medical professional liability insurance coverage you want to purchase, you should understand what is meant by the policy limits. These include:

- Per claim limit—the maximum amount the insurer will pay on your behalf for an individual claim
- Aggregate limit—the maximum amount the insurer will pay on your behalf for all claims during the policy period, usually 1 year

Thus, an ob-gyn who has a $1 million/$3 million policy is covered for up to $1 million in damages for each claim and a total of $3 million in damages for the policy period.

Obstetrics and gynecology is a high-risk specialty for medical liability both in terms of the likelihood of being sued and the size of potential jury awards. This publication cannot recommend the right level of coverage for your situation. However, it may be helpful to know that the 2006 ACOG Survey on Professional Liability found that the typical ob-gyn purchased a policy with limits of $1 million per claim and $3 million annual aggregate.

Important points to remember about coverage or policy limits include the following:

- You will be personally responsible for paying damages that exceed your coverage limits.

- If damages for one claim exceed the limit per claim, you will still have coverage for damages up to that limit if you have another claim until all damages paid on your behalf reach the aggregate limit for the policy period.

- Limits of $1 million/$3 million is the most typical coverage, but you can purchase a policy with lower or higher limits. Premiums will vary accordingly.

- The policy will specify whether it covers your professional corporation and your employees.

- If your professional corporation and employees are covered under the policy, coverage limits may apply to each individual or to the corporation and its employees as a whole.

Try to ensure that your policy covers "ultimate net loss," that is, coverage for defense costs, as well as damages.

Premiums

Insurance carriers consider a variety of factors in setting your premium:

- Your specialty, certification, and experience

- Practice location

- Your claims history (the outcomes and damages paid in any past claims)

Some insurers may offer lower premiums if you are willing to accept a policy with a deductible.

Claims-made policies are initially less expensive than occurrence policies because in the first few years of coverage, the number of potential claims is small. Premiums increase, though, over a period of several years until they reach the "mature" rate:

- The initial premium for a claims-made policy might be quite low—for example, 30% of the mature rate.

- Subsequent annual premiums will probably increase, so be sure to ask what the percentage step increase will be in future years.

Sources of Medical Professional Liability Insurance Coverage

Where do you find medical professional liability insurance? Coverage is available from a variety of sources:

- Commercial companies and mutual companies

- Plans sponsored by state medical societies

- Association-owned (captive) companies (eg, a hospital may form a captive company to provide medical liability insurance to physicians employed on its staff)

- Risk retention groups

- Purchasing groups

An important factor that distinguishes these sources of coverage is the extent to which they are subject to state insurance regulations:

- Commercial and mutual companies, medical society sponsored plans, and captive companies must comply with state requirements for financial solvency and other regulations in all states in which they do business.

- Most states have insurance guaranty funds that provide some coverage to policyholders if an insurer becomes insolvent.

If you obtain coverage from a company regulated by your state's insurance laws and regulations, your state insurance commissioner or department of insurance may be able to assist in resolving any disputes with the insurer.

Nontraditional sources of coverage have emerged in recent years to expand physicians' options for finding medical liability coverage. The tradeoff for the flexibility is that the consumer protection provided by state regulation is less stringent for these types of organizations. For example, a *risk retention group* is a special insurance entity limited to individuals or organizations engaged in similar activities with similar or related liability risk:

- You can recognize this type of organization because it must use "risk retention group" in its name.

- Members must share a common business, trade, or profession. For example, physicians could form a risk retention group for medical liability insurance, and engineers could form a risk retention group, but they could not form a risk retention group together.

- A risk retention group must comply with state insurance laws and regulations only in the state in which it is formed. Risk retention groups frequently incorporate in states with relatively lenient insurance regulations.

- The risk retention group can offer insurance in other states but is not subject to all of another state's laws and regulations.

- Risk retention groups only participate in insurance guaranty funds in the state in which they are licensed. If you purchase liability insurance from a risk retention group licensed in another state and the risk retention group becomes insolvent, you may have limited or no protection.

Purchasing groups do not offer insurance, but instead attempt to provide more economical coverage to physicians by using the power of a larger group to negotiate:

- Purchasing groups buy coverage for members from traditional or non-traditional insurers, including risk retention groups.

- Many state requirements for group insurance do not apply to purchasing groups.

- Purchasing groups are also exempt from states' insurance financial regulation.

You will be paying significant premium dollars to your insurer and relying on that insurer to protect you if you are sued. Find out as much as possible about the carrier from whom you are considering purchasing coverage:

- What type of entity is providing the insurance? A traditional commercial insurer? A captive plan? A risk retention group?

- What state laws, regulations, and consumer protections will apply to your policy?

- Is the carrier financially stable? Will it still be in business 5, 10, or 20 years from now to offer coverage and pay claims?

- How is the carrier regarded by its customers? Talk to other physicians in your community about their experiences with the carrier.

- Check with your state's insurance department to learn about any complaints or problems with the carrier. If you will be purchasing coverage from a risk retention group, check with the state insurance department for the state in which it is licensed.

- Find out what your rights are and where to go if you experience a problem.

Exclusions From Coverage

No medical professional liability insurance policy covers every incident for which you might be sued. The time to find out what your policy does not cover is before you purchase it, not after a claim has been filed. Some of the most common exclusions include the following:

- Punitive damages

- Claims arising from sexual misconduct

- Practicing under the influence of alcohol or illegal drugs

- Antitrust violations

- Criminal or grossly negligent acts

- Libel or slander

- Incidents not involving patient care

- Procedures for which you have not received credentials

- Experimental procedures

- Restraint of trade related to peer review or quality assurance activities

- Prescribing drugs under Investigational New Drug status or not yet approved by the Food and Drug Administration

- Violations of patient confidentiality

In addition, some policies may have other exclusions, such as:

- Liability assumed through a hold-harmless clause in a contract with a health maintenance organization

- Actions by nonphysician employees of the practice

- Practicing outside certain standards of care mandated by the insurer; be sure you know what these are and are comfortable adhering to them

- Defense costs (including attorneys' fees, court reporters' fees, and clerical expenses), which might be excluded or limited

If you are purchasing coverage for less than the full scope of ob-gyn practice (eg, gynecology only), be sure you understand fully the range of procedures and patient care services for which you are covered. A cheap policy could be a poor bargain if its exclusions are very restrictive or do not allow you to practice in the way you feel you should.

Options for Settlement of Claims

If you are sued, the insurer is responsible for paying damages on your behalf and, unless the policy excludes defense costs, can incur considerable legal expenses in defending you. The insurer's overriding interest is to limit its losses. The insurer will be motivated primarily by its financial interest. Your strong feelings that you provided appropriate care and that a bad outcome was not your fault may be of little, if any, consequence to the insurer.

Two clauses that might be included in medical professional liability insurance policies determine how much control the insurer has over the decision to settle a claim:

- "Right to consent to settlement" guarantees that finalizing any agreement to settle the claim must have your consent. Ideally, this is a provision you want to see in your policy; however, increasing numbers of policies written today do not provide this contractual right.

- A "hammer clause" requires that if you do not agree to an insurer's recommendation for settlement, you will be responsible for additional costs if a jury trial results in damages that are higher than the settlement the insurer recommended.

Either of these clauses might appear in options written into your policy. You probably will not see the words "hammer clause." Look for language stating that if you refuse the insurer's recommendation to settle, you will be responsible for defense costs and any damages that exceed the recommended settlement amount. Try to negotiate including a right-to-consent-to-settlement clause and excluding a hammer clause. The time to do this is before you purchase the policy.

Working Effectively With Your Insurer

It is not enough simply to purchase the right coverage for the lowest premium you can find. Making sure your premium dollars are working for you requires some ongoing effort. This section will discuss understanding your insurer's obligations to you, your obligations to the insurer, and your obligations to yourself. You also should review the checklist, "Medical Professional Liability Insurance," in Appendix E.

Insurer Obligations to You

Your medical professional liability insurance policy spells out your insurer's obligations to you. In general, these include:

- Paying any judgment or settlement against you for actions covered by the policy up to the limit specified in the policy

- Investigating a claim

- Negotiating a settlement
- Defending you

The insurer also is obligated to comply with any relevant laws or regulations. These might include requirements about timely notice of nonrenewal or premium increases, as well as requirements to maintain adequate financial reserves.

Your Obligations to the Insurer

In addition to paying your premiums on time, your medical professional liability insurance policy obligates you to work with your insurer in resolving any claim made against you. These obligations begin with notifying the insurer about a claim:

- Your policy may require you to notify your insurer as soon as a claim is filed or as soon as you suspect a claim might be filed.

- You may be concerned that early notification of a possible claim could lead to a premium increase or cancellation of your policy, but there are benefits to early notification:

  —Having more time for evaluation and preparation of a case improves the chances for a successful defense if a claim is actually filed.

  —The insurer and defense attorney can start to collect and record facts and begin evaluating the merits of the case.

  —It may be possible to negotiate an early settlement and avoid the stresses and costs of litigation.

- Remember that any written or recorded information you provide to the insurer is subject to discovery. As soon as your insurer assigns a defense attorney, be sure to direct all communications about the case to the attorney so the information will be protected by attorney–client privilege.

Once a claim has been filed, your policy will require that you cooperate in the defense of your case. If you do not cooperate with the insurer, your coverage could be voided. Developing a good relationship includes the following:

- Try to establish a good rapport with the insurer and your assigned attorney.

- Develop a collegial relationship; this will help ensure that the case is conducted to your satisfaction. It will also avoid adding the unnecessary stress of an adversarial relationship to an already stressful and unpleasant process.

- Be candid and forthcoming about the case from the start. Your attorney will be disadvantaged if surprised by facts you did not disclose at the outset of the case.

You may be concerned that early notification of a possible claim could lead to a premium increase or cancellation of your policy, but there are benefits to early notification.

- Cooperate with and be active in discussions about settling the case. Even if the insurer has the right to settle the case without your consent, most insurers would prefer to have your agreement.

- If you feel pressure to settle the case because of expense, lost practice time, or mental or emotional strain, discuss those issues with the insurer and your attorney.

- Ask for an explanation and justification for any recommended settlement.

- Request the opportunity to concur with any settlement offer even if your policy does not include a right-to-consent-to-settlement clause.

Your Obligations to Yourself

Medical professional liability premiums are a major expense for an ob-gyn. The insurer is not obligated to retain a record of your insurance coverage for as long as the statute of limitations for incidents that occurred while the policy was in effect. In order to protect your investment and to make sure you get the full value of your premium dollars from this large investment, you should:

- Always keep a copy of the policy after it has expired. The policy itself is the best proof that you were insured if you are sued and the insurer does not have a record of your coverage.

- Keep a record of all communications with your carrier.

- Find out about your insurer's appeal process.

- Learn about any special discounts or credits available for participation in your carrier's risk management program.

Although your insurer will assign a defense attorney to your case, you may wonder whether you should hire your own attorney—one who is accountable only to you, not to your insurer. There are some circumstances when hiring personal defense counsel is a good idea:

- Inadequate coverage—If the insurer believes your policy limits are not adequate, the insurer will inform you that you have the right to hire your own attorney at your expense to protect personal financial exposure.

- Reservation of rights—If there is any question about whether you were insured for a procedure or whether the policy was in effect, the insurer will send you a letter agreeing to defend you but reserving the right to contest the coverage issue after the case is resolved.

- Conflict of interest—In the event that codefendants are insured by the same liability insurance company and the interests of the respective insureds are adverse to one another, an insurer will typically assign separate and independant counsel to each party-defendant. In the event of an insurer's refusal to do so, it would be strongly advised to retain separate counsel.

In any of these situations, hiring your own defense attorney is a wise investment. If you have "ultimate net loss" coverage instead of "pure loss" coverage, you might be able to recover some expenses of hiring your own attorney.

Protecting Your Assets

If a patient wins a judgment against you with damages higher than the limits of your medical professional liability insurance coverage, your assets can be seized and liquidated to pay the damages. Every ob-gyn should have a plan for protecting personal assets. Adequate medical professional liability, business, and other insurance should form the foundation of this plan. However, you should also consider additional strategies for protecting assets in the event of a judgment higher than your coverage limits. This section provides a brief overview of principles and options for asset protection. For a more detailed discussion of this topic, see ACOG's publication *The Business of Medicine: An Essential Guide for Obstetrician–Gynecologists,* published in 2005.

Principles of Asset Protection

The major goal of an asset protection plan is to transfer assets to forms that are exempt from, or offer some legal protection from, seizure and liquidation to satisfy a judgment against you. Remember three fundamental points about asset protection:

1. An asset protection plan must be a long-term strategy. Plan in advance and implement your plan promptly.

2. You cannot protect assets after a claim has been filed or an event occurs that makes a claim likely (eg, wrong-site surgery).

3. Consulting an attorney and financial advisor knowledgeable about asset protection in your state is a must.

Property Exempt From Seizure

The amounts and types of your property that would be protected from being seized to pay damages in a medical liability judgment against you depend on where you live. Exemptions could include the following:

- The Employee Retirement Income Security Act (ERISA) qualified pension funds such as 401(k) and 403(b)

- Individual retirement accounts, Keoghs, and other non-ERISA retirement accounts

- Insurance and annuities

- Social Security payments

- Wages

- Your primary residence (The value of the homestead exemption ranges from nothing in some states to an unlimited amount in Florida and Texas.)

- Assets that are given away, including gifts to certain trusts, as long as the transfer is not fraudulent

Treatment of the types of assets listed above varies significantly from state to state, so consult with local experts.

Trusts

Assets you place in a trust are held and controlled by another person, the trustee, on behalf of your designated beneficiary. Examples of types of trusts that may offer some protection for your assets include:

- An irrevocable trust, which cannot be terminated, offers asset protection if the creator of the trust is not the sole trustee. This means, for example, that you cannot shield assets in an irrevocable trust for your children unless someone else has sole control or shares control with you.

- An offshore protection trust offers strong asset protection. To establish this type of trust, you would transfer assets to a trust subject to the laws of another country that does not necessarily honor judgments granted outside its own courts. Offshore trusts must be carefully drafted and can be expensive to set up and maintain.

- A spendthrift trust prevents the beneficiary from transferring his or her interests in the assets to someone else and also prevents a creditor, such as someone who has won a judgment against you, from gaining access to the assets. In some states, if you create the trust, you can also be a beneficiary.

- A qualified person residence trust places your home in a trust for a specific period of time, but allows you to live in it for that time. After that time period, the home belongs to the beneficiaries of the trust.

Other Strategies

Other strategies for protecting assets include the following:

- Form a business entity such as a corporation, limited partnership, or limited liability company for your practice. This can protect business assets from claims against you and can protect your assets from claims against the business.

- Transfer income-producing assets (eg, securities, investment real estate) to a family limited partnership to protect income-producing assets such as securities or investment real estate.

- Divide assets with your spouse.

- Borrow against exposed assets and place the proceeds in exempted assets.

This discussion is intended to encourage you to begin thinking about a plan for protecting your assets. All the strategies mentioned involve a complex set of tradeoffs. Consult with qualified legal and financial professionals to establish a plan that is right for you.

Coping With a Crisis in Your Medical Professional Liability Coverage

An ob-gyn learns that her medical professional liability premium will double for the next year and the payment is due in 60 days. Worse yet, a colleague in the community learns that his policy will not be renewed. These stories have become all too familiar in the past few years. To cope with an unaffordable premium hike or policy cancellation, a few strategies may help:

- Try to salvage the situation

  —File an appeal with the insurer. Become familiar with your carrier's process for appealing unreasonable premium increases or nonrenewal decisions before you are faced with a crisis.

  —Enlist the help of your state insurance commissioner. The insurance department may be able to mandate an emergency extension of your coverage if the policy has been cancelled. Use the extra time to explore other options for coverage.

- Reduce coverage limits

  —Determine whether coverage limits are mandated by state law, hospital staff bylaws, and managed care contracts. If not, lower your per claim and aggregate limits to reduce your premium.

  —Find out whether your carrier or another carrier will offer a lower premium if you have a deductible. This would require you to pay all damages up to the amount of the deductible.

  —Make sure your personal asset protection plan is strong if you lower your coverage limits. You assume more risk in the event of a successful claim against you.

- Explore other sources of coverage

  —As an ACOG Fellow or Junior Fellow, you have access to the services of an insurance broker who can help you find insurers writing coverage in your state.

  —As a last resort, if you cannot find insurance from conventional sources, look into secondary market insurers, also known as "surplus lines." Be aware, though, that coverage in the secondary market will probably be significantly more expensive.

- Change your employment situation

  —Your hospital may be able to provide coverage. You may have to become an employee or contractor of the hospital to avoid trouble with laws banning kickbacks and self referrals (see Glossary, Stark I and II). Consult an attorney before launching an arrangement with the hospital.

  —Think about affiliating with a larger group. Some very large groups may have established their own captive plans; others may be able to negotiate for lower premiums.

Become familiar with your carrier's process for appealing unreasonable premium increases or nonrenewal decisions before you are faced with a crisis.

—Make use of ACOG's Career Connection to explore other job opportunities (see www.acog.org).

If all else fails and you decide to relocate or close your practice, you will need to obtain tail coverage unless you had an occurrence policy. You will also need to provide patients with adequate notice to avoid charges of patient abandonment. (See Chapter 7, "Patient Communication," for a discussion on terminating the physician–patient relationship.)

Consider Changing Your Practice

If your efforts to obtain other coverage or negotiate a lower premium are unsuccessful, you might consider cutting back or eliminating clinical activities that contribute to your high premium:

- Reduce your risk by cutting back on high-risk obstetric care or reducing the number of deliveries you perform.

- Drop obstetrics altogether.

- Cut back on major gynecologic surgery.

- Practice only office-based ambulatory gynecology.

Any of these actions could lead to a substantial reduction in your premium. However, these actions probably will also significantly reduce your practice revenue, so consult with your business advisor before making any drastic changes. Consider whether you will derive the same satisfaction and professional challenge from an altered practice.

Forgoing Insurance or "Going Bare"

Faced with medical professional liability premiums of $100,000 or more, some ob-gyns wonder whether, at these prices, buying insurance is a good deal. Would it be better to save premium dollars and, in effect, self-insure for medical liability? A number of issues should be considered and addressed before deciding to practice without medical liability insurance or "going bare":

- What is the environment for protection of personal assets in your state? Is your home protected? What about your spouse's assets or assets of your practice? Retirement funds? Children's college savings?

- Do state laws or regulations require that you carry medical liability insurance?

- Do agreements with health insurers require you to carry medical liability insurance? Would you be able to renegotiate those agreements?

- Do the hospitals at which you practice require that you be insured?

Practicing without insurance will probably be feasible for only a few ob-gyns. If you are considering this alternative, you should seek competent guidance from a qualified attorney and financial advisor.

Special Medical Professional Liability Issues for Residents

If you are an ob-gyn resident, you are no doubt acutely aware of the medical professional liability risks facing anyone who has chosen to become an obstetrician–gynecologist. Although you may not yet need to find and purchase your own medical liability insurance policy, the topics discussed so far in this chapter are still relevant. Within a few years, you will undertake the task of finding your own insurance, so mastering the basics now will make that job easier. In addition, there are specific insurance-related issues for residents that could affect your ability to practice in the future. This section will provide you with a checklist for medical liability insurance coverage during residency and will discuss coverage limits and restrictions, as well as future considerations for residents.

Checklist for Medical Professional Liability Insurance During Residency

As a resident, you probably have little control over the medical professional liability insurance coverage available to you. The residency program provides the coverage and there is little, if any, room to negotiate. Answering the following questions will help you gather the information you need to understand the coverage you have as a resident and what you may need to do to keep future options open. The Accreditation Council on Graduate Medical Education (ACGME) requires institutions sponsoring residency programs to provide occurrence medical liability insurance coverage for residents. However, you should confirm the details of your coverage yourself:

- What type of coverage do you have, occurrence or claims-made?

- If you leave the residency program, will you be covered for incidents that occurred while you were in the program?

- What are the limits of your coverage? The program might not be able to tell you your individual per claim and aggregate limits because the program may have a large combined aggregate. If that is the case, the program should be able to tell you the combined aggregate.

- Is tail coverage paid for by the residency program? If so, what are the limits and how are they applied? If not, will you be able to purchase tail coverage when you complete residency?

- Are there any limitations on practice included in the policy?

- Will claims filed during residency affect your ability to obtain insurance after residency?

Obtain copies of the residency program's medical liability insurance policies for each year you are in the program. Keep documentation of coverage indefinitely:

- You could be sued for an incident that occurred during residency long after you completed the program and long after the residency program discarded its records. Be sure you have proof of coverage.

If you have been named in multiple medical liability claims while a resident, you may be affected by surcharging or experience rating.

- If your residency program is self-insured, assuming all risk for medical liability claims, obtain and keep a written statement or certificate of the coverage provided.

If your residency program is self-insured, but has reinsurance from an outside insurer for claims above a specified level, obtain documentation of both policies.

Restrictions on Coverage

In addition to the types of coverage restrictions discussed above, residents may face other restrictions. For example, almost all coverage provided by residency programs excludes moonlighting activities from coverage. If you are thinking about practicing part time at another institution, make sure you are covered:

- Ask whether you will be covered under the medical liability insurance policy for the institution where you are moonlighting.

- If not, purchase medical liability insurance to cover your moonlighting activities.

- If you purchase claims-made coverage, look into the cost of also purchasing the tail coverage for your moonlighting. Future costs could outweigh the current benefit of extra income.

Future Considerations: Surcharging or Experience Rating

Even if your residency program provides occurrence coverage or pays for your tail coverage, you cannot count on being able to complete residency and enter practice with a clean slate from a medical professional liability insurance carrier's point of view. Plaintiff's attorneys frequently file claims against all health care professionals whose names appear on the patient's medical record, including residents. If you have been named in multiple medical liability claims while a resident, you may be affected by surcharging or experience rating:

- *Surcharging* or *experience rating* is the practice of assessing higher premiums for physicians who have had medical liability claims against them.

- Insurers who surcharge assess points against a physician based on the number of claims filed, the outcome of the claims, and the amount of damages or settlement.

- After the physician's points reach a certain threshold, the insurer charges a premium higher than the usual for the specialty.

If you have had claims, look into whether insurers in the areas you wish to practice surcharge or experience rate. If insurance in certain areas will be very expensive or hard to obtain, it is better to have that information at the beginning of your job search, rather than several weeks before you are due to begin a new practice.

Purchasing medical liability insurance is one of the most expensive and most important decisions you will make in your career as an ob-gyn. The best tool for protecting your interests now and in the future is information. Learn as much as you can about the options for obtaining coverage, the benefits and disadvantages of different types of coverage, and the provisions of the policy you select.

KEY POINTS

✓ Occurrence policies are favorable for ob-gyns because they cover events that happen while the policy is in effect, regardless of when the claim is filed.

✓ Claims-made policies only provide coverage if both the incident and the claim filing happen while the policy is in effect, though not necessarily in the same policy year.

✓ If you have claims-made coverage and change insurers or leave practice, you must obtain reporting endorsement ("tail") or prior acts ("nose") coverage.

✓ Claims-made policies are initially cheaper than occurrence policies, but premiums can rise sharply.

✓ Learn as much as you can about your coverage and your insurer before you buy the policy.

✓ Every ob-gyn should have a plan for protecting personal assets. Consult with a qualified financial advisor.

Chapter 11

Coping With the Stress of a Medical Professional Liability Claim

Nearly 90% of all ACOG Fellows who responded to the 2006 ACOG Survey on Professional Liability indicated they had at least one claim filed against them during their professional careers. Being sued for medical liability can be one of the most stressful life events a physician experiences. If you have not been sued yet, you should know what to expect if and when you are sued and how to support a colleague who has been sued. If you are currently involved in litigation, you should understand the sources of stress and how to cope. If you have been sued in the past, you need to recognize the effect the experience may have had on you and your family. (See "Resources" at the end of this chapter for information on coping with litigation stress.)

This chapter discusses:

- Why a medical professional liability suit is so stressful

- Recognizing common symptoms of litigation stress

- Strategies for coping with stress

- What to do when the case is over

- Helping a colleague who has been sued

Why a Medical Professional Liability Suit Is So Stressful

The nature of a medical professional liability claim virtually guarantees that a physician who is being sued will undergo tremendous stress. The plaintiff seeks compensation; for compensation to be paid, fault must be proved. Your attorney and insurer may say the claim is about compensation, not your competence, but it probably does not feel that way to you. The trust you worked hard to establish with the patient has been breached. At its heart, the medical liability claim accuses you of failing to do your job.

People who successfully apply to and complete medical school and demanding ob-gyn training tend to share a number of personality traits:

- You set high expectations for yourself and demand your best effort.

- You are hardworking and conscientious.

You are accustomed to and comfortable with being in charge, but the legal system is not under your control. It is an alien environment, very unlike medicine.

- You are somewhat compulsive in your attention to detail.
- You are directive and like to be in charge.

Medical school and residency training reinforce and intensify these traits. If you are like most ob-gyns, being a physician is not a job, it is the core of who you are. Your high standards and willingness to accept responsibility help you succeed as a physician. These traits serve your patients well, but make coping with a medical liability lawsuit especially stressful:

- You have worked hard and sacrificed to gain your skills; you are justifiably proud of what you have accomplished.
- The lawsuit represents a challenge to your competence, integrity, and self-concept.
- You may feel you have been labeled a failure, a bad doctor.
- You might worry that everything you have worked for is at risk.

Both the legal system itself and the litigation process create stress for most physicians. You are accustomed to and comfortable with being in charge, but the legal system is not under your control. It is an alien environment, very unlike medicine:

- Medicine is collegial; the legal system is adversarial.
- Medicine values promptness and rapid resolution of problems; delays are an unavoidable element of the legal system.

The litigation process is very unpredictable with many stops and starts. Most physicians prefer to confront a problem, deal with it promptly, and move on, but litigation can stretch on for a very lengthy time period. In fact, an ob-gyn medical liability case takes an average of 3–4 years to be resolved. Lack of resolution for such a long time is highly stressful on its own.

Recognizing Common Symptoms of Litigation Stress

By now you may have some idea of the steps in the litigation process (claim filing, discovery, trial, settlement, etc.), but you may not know what emotions you might experience when served with a lawsuit. Research shows that nearly all physicians who are sued experience emotional distress that can come and go throughout the litigation process. Most physicians experience:

- Initial shock and denial
- Anger
- Anxiety about the professional and financial impact of the case
- Feelings of loss of control
- Frustration
- Difficulty concentrating
- Insomnia

It also would not be uncommon to experience symptoms of any of the following:

- Major depressive disorder

- Adjustment disorder

- New physical illness, or recurrence or exacerbation of previous illness

Strategies for Coping With Stress

Managing the stress that comes with litigation is essential for your mental and physical health, your family's well-being, and a successful defense. Coping with litigation-related stress is also a risk management issue:

- Difficulty in concentrating, irritability, or anger can make you more vulnerable to incidents likely to trigger another claim.

- Physicians who are sued are at twice the usual risk for an additional claim within the next year.

Most physicians are task-oriented individuals who feel better when they are actively involved in solving a problem. Taking action to defend yourself against the charges in the case might help to relieve some stress:

- Identify those aspects of the litigation process that you can control or at least influence.

- Take an active role in your defense.

- Learn as much as you can about the process and how your case will be conducted.

- Review the scientific and clinical issues relevant to your case, but do not alter the medical record.

- Suggest names of appropriate experts to your defense team, but do not contact candidates yourself. Your lawyers may select someone else. Do not be offended as long as the expert is well qualified.

Remember that the litigation process is unpredictable and lengthy. You probably will be faced with periods of hectic activity related to the case followed by stretches of time when nothing seems to be happening at all. Being mentally prepared for the delays, cancellations, and uneven pace of the litigation process will help you cope.

Even while you devote energy and time to your defense, you must continue to function as a physician. Doing whatever you can to gain a greater sense of control over your work should help to reduce your stress:

- Cut back on work hours or the number of patients you see, if possible.

- Reduce your involvement in areas of practice you find stressful or anxiety producing.

- Focus more time and energy on the areas of practice you enjoy.

- Do not get involved in activities that compromise your standards.

- Find time for activities that improve your skills and bolster your confidence.

The most difficult task of all may be to compartmentalize—that is, to prevent worries about your liability case from invading other areas of your life. If your case is typical, a few years could pass before the case is resolved, so you will need to find ways to put it out of your mind, at least temporarily, in order to function effectively.

For most medical families, a medical professional liability lawsuit results in a significant personal crisis for everyone involved—physician, spouse, and other family members. Communicating as much as you can with family members about the nonconfidential aspects of the lawsuit—the allegations, possible publicity, and expected testimony—can help to reduce feelings of isolation. Your children may have questions and concerns about the case. Answer any questions as honestly as you can, keeping in mind your child's age and ability to understand the information. Other tactics can help:

- Schedule more leisure time. Take a vacation if possible.

- Spend more time with your family and friends.

- Get regular exercise.

- Limit chemical or alcohol use.

- If you have neglected financial planning, address this; it will help relieve some worries about your family's future.

- Ask for help in dealing with the stress of litigation; this is not an admission of weakness or professional incompetence.

- Do not try to diagnose and treat your own symptoms—even "just" insomnia.

- See your primary care physician for a thorough evaluation of any symptoms you experience. If you do not have a primary care physician, find one.

Legal concerns might discourage you from talking about your feelings about the case with anyone, but it is important to find social support from family, friends, and colleagues. Reach out for the help you need, but take common sense precautions:

- Talk with your attorney about your need to discuss the case. Find out what types of discussions might be protected and what would be riskier.

- Do not discuss the case with anyone who is involved or who might be called as a witness.

- Limit any discussions of the details involved in the case to conversations with your attorney. The purpose of talking with family or colleagues is to get emotional support, not legal advice.

Obtaining help from a mental health professional or organized support group also can be very beneficial. However, it is important to consider their legal status:

- Some states treat conversations with a mental health professional or your doctor as privileged communications. Find out the status in your state.

- Ask your insurer about any support services available for defendant physicians. Your state medical society also may sponsor litigation support groups.

- Courts might recognize support groups' confidentiality pledges, but frequently do not.

- Be sure to discuss with your attorney the advisability of and legal protections for participation in a support group.

What To Do When the Case Is Over: Moving On!

Whether you are dropped from the case, settle, or proceed to trial, win or lose, getting back to normal may not be easy. You might be angry at the time and energy lost in defending what you felt was a groundless claim. You may feel reluctant to take on certain types of patients or procedures. Relationships with and trust in colleagues might have suffered. Symptoms of depression, emotional problems, or stress-related physical illness may persist. If you lost the case, you may feel isolated from the medical community.

One way to begin to regain a sense of control is to choose to use the painful experience of being sued as an opportunity for learning and personal growth:

- What are your priorities? Does the way you spend your time and energy match your priorities?

- Did the case identify areas in which you could improve, for example, strengthening your documentation and informed consent practices?

- Put the case in perspective with the rest of your professional life. Identify your strengths and accomplishments.

- Work hard to overcome any negative attitudes toward patients or medical practice that might have grown out of your experience with litigation. Get counseling if necessary.

Helping a Colleague Who Has Been Sued

Many physicians who are involved in medical professional liability litigation feel alone and isolated from the medical community. Your silence in the face of a friend's crisis could send a message that you think he or she is a bad doctor. If you know that a colleague has been sued, reach out to offer your support:

- Express sympathy.

- Ask how you can help.

- Be alert for persistent signs of depression or other symptoms suggesting the need for professional intervention.

- Encourage your colleague to seek help and support for him or herself and family.

KEY POINTS

✓ Being sued for medical professional liability is a common experience for ob-gyns. Even the best, most skilled physicians can be sued.

✓ A medical professional liability case presents a crisis for the ob-gyn and his or her family.

✓ The stress resulting from a medical liability case can have a negative effect on your personal and professional life, and your ability to defend yourself against the charge.

✓ As an ob-gyn, you must be prepared for the probability that you will be sued.

✓ Learn to recognize the symptoms of stress, develop coping strategies, and seek the help you need.

Resources

American College of Obstetricians and Gynecologists. From exam room to courtroom: navigating litigation and coping with stress [CD-ROM]. Washington, DC: ACOG; 2006.

Coping with the stress of medical professional liability litigation. ACOG Committee Opinion No. 406. American College of Obstetricians and Gynecologists, May 2008.

Charles SC, Frish PR. Adverse events, stress, and litigation. New York (NY): Oxford University Press; 2005.

Chapter 12

Government Requirements Affecting Medical Practice

Many federal and state laws and regulations affect practicing physicians. Failure to follow government requirements could carry heavy financial penalties and expose you to criminal prosecution. Inform yourself about the regulations that apply to your practice and make sure you are in compliance.

This chapter provides a brief overview of several significant federal laws and regulations likely to affect you as you practice obstetrics and gynecology:

- Emergency Medical Treatment and Active Labor Act (EMTALA)

- Health Insurance Portability and Accountability Act (HIPAA)

- Fraud and abuse

- Civil Rights Act

- Americans With Disabilities Act (ADA)

- Occupational Safety and Health Administration (OSHA)

- Clinical Laboratory Improvement Amendments of 1988 (CLIA)

Emergency Medical Treatment and Active Labor Act

Congress enacted EMTALA to ensure that everyone who seeks medical help from a hospital emergency department receives appropriate screening and treatment, regardless of his or her ability to pay. All hospitals participating in Medicare must meet these requirements, so chances are that your hospital must comply with EMTALA. The law's requirements for on-call physicians may also affect you.

Be sure you understand your obligations and your hospital's EMTALA procedures; consequences for EMTALA violations are serious. Although EMTALA is not directly related to medical tort liability, the fact that you or the hospital broke the EMTALA rules could be very damaging to your defense of a civil action alleging medical negligence.

Congress enacted EMTALA to ensure that everyone who seeks medical help from a hospital emergency department receives appropriate screening and treatment, regardless of his or her ability to pay.

Patient Screening

All hospitals that participate in the Medicare program and have a dedicated emergency department must comply with EMTALA's requirements for patient screening and transfer. The regulations define a dedicated emergency department as any department or facility of the hospital that meets one of the following criteria:

- It is licensed by the state as an emergency room or emergency department.

- The hospital presents the facility or department to the public as available to provide care for emergency medical conditions without an appointment.

- In the previous year it provided at least one third of its entire outpatient visits for urgent treatment of emergency medical conditions.

Labor and delivery units and psychiatry departments can meet these criteria and, therefore, be covered by EMTALA.

Anyone who requests an examination or treatment for a medical condition at the hospital must be provided a screening examination without regard to his or her ability to pay. This requirement is not limited to patients who come to the emergency room. In general, anyone who requests an examination or treatment for an emergency medical condition anywhere on the hospital property is entitled to EMTALA's protections.

As a medical staff member or an ob-gyn resident, you may be asked to perform a screening to find out whether a patient has an "emergency medical condition." The Emergency Medical Treatment and Active Labor Act defines an emergency medical condition as a condition with symptoms severe enough that, if the patient does not receive immediate care, you have a reasonable expectation that one of the following consequences could occur:

- Her health would be in serious jeopardy.

- She would experience serious impairment of a bodily function.

- She would experience serious dysfunction of a bodily organ or part.

Special requirements apply for screening pregnant women in the emergency room:

- You must consider the health of the fetus in deciding whether a pregnant patient has an emergency medical condition.

- A pregnant patient having contractions is in "true labor" and, therefore, must be determined to have an emergency medical condition unless a physician, certified nurse midwife, or other qualified medical professional certifies that she is in false labor.

- A pregnant patient having contractions also has an emergency medical condition if transferring her to another facility would threaten her health or her fetus' health.

- If you have observed the patient and diagnosed false labor, she does not have an emergency medical condition.

- If you determine that a pregnant patient having contractions has an emergency medical condition, EMTALA considers that she is not stabilized until the baby and placenta are delivered.

The hospital can determine whether a physician must perform screening examinations or whether another type of health care provider is qualified. For example, your hospital could decide that nurses or nurse practitioners may perform some screenings.

If you find that a patient has an emergency medical condition, you have two options depending on the circumstances and your hospital's capabilities:

1. Treat and stabilize the patient.

2. Transfer the patient to another hospital that is better able to provide the necessary care.

Criteria for Transferring Patients

Most of the time, EMTALA prohibits you from transferring an unstable patient. However, you can transfer an unstable patient to another hospital under the following conditions:

- She requests the transfer. She must be informed of her rights to stay at the hospital, along with the risks and benefits of transfer, including the fact that she is not medically stable. The request must be documented in writing.

- Your hospital does not have the facilities or personnel to provide the care she needs. You must sign a statement certifying that the benefits of transfer are greater than the risks.

If you recommend transfer to another hospital, but the patient refuses, take the following steps:

- Inform the patient of the benefits of the transfer and the risks of remaining at your hospital.

- Include in the medical record a description of the proposed transfer and your reason(s) for recommending the transfer.

- Make every reasonable attempt to document in writing the patient's informed refusal of the transfer.

Interhospital Care and Transport System

Your hospital will have a system and procedure set up for transferring and receiving patients. All facilities involved in the system must work together to specify how they will accomplish the following:

- Comply with relevant local, state, and federal regulations.

- Obtain informed consent before moving the patient.

If you are transferring a patient to another facility, your hospital is responsible for the patient until she arrives at the receiving hospital.

- Develop formal agreements outlining each hospital's procedures and responsibilities for patient care.

- Provide patient identification during transport.

- Use patient care orders, guidelines, and verbal communication during transport.

- Educate staff at all facilities about the interhospital care and transport system.

Make sure you are familiar with the interhospital care and transport system your hospital uses.

Referring Hospital Responsibilities

If you are transferring a patient to another facility, your hospital is responsible for the patient until she arrives at the receiving hospital. Obligations include the following:

- Evaluating and stabilizing the patient

- Assuring that the receiving hospital has adequate space and qualified staff to treat the patient

- Providing all available medical records

Receiving Hospital Responsibilities

If your hospital receives patients from other facilities, your institution is responsible for coordinating the transport system and making sure transferred patients are provided appropriate care. Receiving hospitals must have plans in place to prevent bed shortages. A receiving hospital cannot refuse a transfer if it has space and qualified staff available.

Transport Team

The transport team must be capable of providing supportive care for a broad range of emergency conditions. It should be able to:

- Provide staff and vehicles on very short notice

- Communicate during transport with the receiving hospital

- Coordinate both air and ground transport

- Maintain the equipment needed for safely transporting patients (eg, physiologic function monitors, resuscitation and support equipment, medical gas tanks)

- Support electrical equipment

Air Transport

Many patient transfers take place through air transport. Medical equipment on board helicopters and airplanes can develop mechanical problems during flight and endanger the patient. Transport teams should test their equipment regularly.

Assistance in choosing and testing medical equipment for air transport is available from:

- The U.S. Army Aeromedical Research Laboratory, Fort Rucker, Alabama (http://www.usaarl.army.mil/)

- Armstrong Laboratory, Brooks City-Base, Texas (http://www.brooks.af.mil/)

- Association of Air Medical Services, Pasadena, California (http://www.aams.org/)

- Emergency Care Research Institute (ECRI), Plymouth Meeting, Pennsylvania (http://www.ecri.org/)

- Federal Aviation Administration, Washington, DC (http://www.faa.gov/)

Your EMTALA Obligations

The Emergency Medical Treatment and Active Labor Act requires that hospitals make available to the emergency room all the specialties represented on its staff. Not all specialties must be on call at all times, but the hospital must have policies in place to address situations in which no one from a particular specialty is on call. As part of your hospital medical staff responsibilities, you may be required to be on call for the emergency room. If so, be sure you understand your EMTALA obligations:

- When on call, you must respond to the hospital's request to screen or treat a patient in a timely manner.

- You cannot refuse to see a patient or refuse to accept a transfer if you are capable of caring for the patient.

- You may be on call for more than one hospital at the same time.

- You may schedule elective surgery during hours on call.

- You cannot ask to have a patient transferred to your office or another hospital for your convenience.

- You must find a replacement if you cannot be available for your scheduled hours on call.

EMTALA Enforcement

Penalties for hospitals and physicians who fail to meet their obligations under EMTALA are severe fines of up to $50,000 per violation and exclusion from the Medicare program. If you report an EMTALA violation or refuse to transfer an unstable patient, the hospital cannot penalize you.

Health Insurance Portability and Accountability Act

When Congress adopted HIPAA in 1996, the law was known primarily for its provisions providing stronger health insurance protections for people leaving jobs and people with preexisting medical conditions. Now, though, when physicians talk about HIPAA, they are most likely thinking about its provisions that have a significant influence on day-to-day medical practice operations:

- Transactions and code sets

- Security

- Privacy of individually identifiable health information

If your practice stores or transmits patient health information electronically, you must comply with these three sets of HIPAA regulations.

Transactions and Code Sets

The transactions and code sets rules implement provisions of HIPAA intended to standardize and simplify how health information is stored and submitted in electronic formats. The goal is to make it easier for you to submit health insurance claims and for health insurers to process and pay those claims by having everyone format information in a uniform way. October 16, 2003, was the deadline for final implementation of the transactions and code sets rules. Some insurers may still accept noncompliant claims, although eventually payment probably will be denied.

If you have not done so already, work with your software vendor and billing clearinghouse to make sure your claims comply with the transactions and code sets rules. You can obtain a free copy of *ACOG's Transactions and Code Sets Compliance Manual* at http://www.gatesmoore.com/transaction_&_codesets-standards.HIPAA.ACOG.html.

Security

Electronic storage of patients' personal health information raises some significant concerns about unauthorized release of that information. If you store patient health information electronically, you will need to comply with the HIPAA security regulations, effective April 21, 2005. The rules include:

- Electronic signature requirements

- Physical storage safeguards

- Transmission safeguards

- Access safeguards

You will have some flexibility in implementing the rules in your practice. While you are required to implement some of the standards, others are considered "addressable." If a standard is addressable, you will be able to:

- Determine whether it is reasonable and appropriate for your practice

- Substitute another measure

- Document why the standard is not appropriate for your practice

To assist you in complying with the HIPAA security rules, ACOG has developed the *HIPAA Security Manual*, available free of charge on the members-only portion of the ACOG web site (http://www.acog.org/departments/dept_web.cfm?recno=35).

Privacy of Individually Identifiable Health Information

Safeguarding the privacy and confidentiality of a patient's personal health information is an ethical obligation for ob-gyns (see Appendix D, "Code of Professional Ethics of the American College of Obstetricians and Gynecologists") and a legal requirement. You also are subject to HIPAA's privacy regulation if you or your employer or practice conduct any of the following activities electronically:

- Submitting claims

- Checking a patient's eligibility or coverage

- Requesting preauthorization or a referral

- Receiving payments, notices of payments, or explanation of benefits

If you conduct certain transactions electronically, you are a covered entity. The HIPAA privacy regulations cover all forms of protected health information (PHI)—paper, electronic, and oral. Covered entities must do the following:

- Develop a written privacy policy for your practice.

- Designate a privacy officer who will be responsible for implementing the privacy policy. If your practice is small, this will probably be an existing staff person.

- Train all practice staff on the privacy policy.

- Provide all patients with a written Notice of Privacy Rights and Practices, which both explains a patient's privacy rights and outlines how your practice will use her protected health information.

- Make a good faith effort to obtain the patient's written acknowledgment of receiving the notice.

- Obtain contracts with business associates with whom you share protected health information that provide assurance the business associate will protect the information.

- Limit disclosures of protected health information to the minimum amount necessary.

- Take reasonable precautions to prevent accidental disclosure of protected health information.

HIPAA does *not* require you to do the following:

- Obtain the patient's consent for disclosures of protected health information related to treatment, payment, or operations.

- Make significant physical modifications to your office.

- Limit the amount of clinically relevant information you provide to others caring for your patients.

Under HIPAA, a patient has the right to inspect her protected health information and to request that you correct any inaccuracies. You are not required to honor her request, but you must provide a written justification for refusal. You must ask for a patient's consent to disclose her protected health information for purposes other than treatment, payment, or operations. Penalties for violating the HIPAA privacy regulations include:

- $100 per incident for accidental disclosure of protected health information, up to a maximum of $25,000 per year

- Up to $250,000 and 10 years in prison for intentional misuse of PHI

Detailed information about the privacy regulations is available at http://www.hhs.gov/ocr/hipaa/. ACOG members also have access to additional resources on HIPAA compliance at http://www.acog.org/departments/dept_web.cfm?recno=35.

HIPAA and the National Provider Identifier

The National Provider Identifier (NPI) is a unique, permanent identification number for health care providers who bill for their services. The NPI remains with the provider despite job or location changes. All HIPAA covered health care providers, health plans, and clearinghouses must use the NPI in the administrative and financial transactions adopted under HIPAA.

If you do not already have an NPI number, you can obtain yours online through the National Plan and Provider Enumeration System (NPPES) pages on CMS's web site http://nppes.cms.hhs.gov/NPPES/Welcome.do.

The NPI is a 10-digit number. The numbers do not convey specific information about health care providers, such as the state in which they live or their medical specialty. Since May 23, 2007, the NPI must be used for all electronic transactions instead of the individual legacy provider identifiers in the HIPAA standards transactions.

The HIPAA requires covered providers to share their NPI with other providers, health plans, clearinghouses, and any entity that may need it for billing purposes. The NPI Registry is an online database of provider information that is accessible from the CMS web site to assist in the sharing of a provider's NPI information (http://nppes.cms.hhs.gov/NPPES/NPIRegistryHome.do).

Fraud and Abuse

The business side of medical practice offers unscrupulous individuals many chances to abuse the health care system for their own gain. Health care fraud and abuse usually involve billing for services that were not provided and billing for services that were not medically necessary. Protect yourself from any allegations of fraud and abuse with the following:

- Accurately document the services you provide.

- Ensure that coding accurately represents the services you provided and that documentation supports the codes that appear on the bill.

- Perform only reasonable and necessary services.

Several federal and criminal statutes apply to health care fraud and abuse. Consult with qualified legal counsel if you believe any of these might affect your practice.

False Claims Acts

Two of the federal government's main weapons in its efforts to fight fraud and abuse in the Medicare and Medicaid programs are the criminal and civil False Claims Acts. If you knowingly submit a fraudulent claim to a federal health care program (eg, Medicare or Medicaid), you violate the False Claims Act:

- If convicted under the criminal False Claims Act, you could be sentenced to prison for up to 5 years and be subject to a fine.

- Civil penalties include damages three times the amount of the fraudulent claims, plus $5,000–$10,000 fines for each fraudulent claim filed.

Antikickback Statute

The purpose of the Antikickback Statute is to ensure that health care providers make decisions about patient referrals on the basis of what is in a patient's best interest, not on the basis of possible financial gain. Under the Antikickback Statute, the following actions are criminal:

- Knowingly paying or receiving anything of value in exchange for referring a federal health care program beneficiary to a particular health care provider or supplier

- Offering inducements directly to beneficiaries to persuade them to choose one provider or supplier over another

Penalties for violating the Antikickback Statute are severe and include:

- Felony conviction

- Criminal fines up to $25,000

- Imprisonment for up to 5 years

- Civil money penalties up to $50,000

- Exclusion from federal health care programs

Many legitimate and beneficial business arrangements common within health care (eg, hospital recruitment of physicians to underserved areas) could violate the Antikickback Statute. Congress authorized the Department of Health and Human Services to designate specific business and payment practices as *safe harbors*: a business arrangement that violates the Antikickback Statute, but that the Office of the Inspector General has defined in regulations as one that will not be prosecuted. You can find the descriptions of the safe harbors the Inspector General has designated at http://www.oig.hhs.gov/fraud/safeharborregulations.html. If you are thinking about a business arrangement with another health provider—for exam-

Under the Antikickback Statute, it is a crime to knowingly pay or receive anything of value in exchange for referring a federal health care program beneficiary to a particular health care provider or supplier.

ple, you are negotiating to lease office space from a hospital—be sure your attorney reviews the proposed agreement with the Antikickback Statute in mind.

Self-Referral Prohibitions

The federal statutes governing the Medicare and Medicaid programs prohibit you from referring patients to a health care provider in which you or an immediate family member has a financial interest. You probably know these prohibitions as the Stark regulations (see Glossary). The intent of the Stark rules is similar to the intent of the Antikickback Statute—to prevent a patient from being steered to a specific provider because her physician will profit from that referral.

The self-referral prohibition applies to a specific list of designated health services:

- Clinical laboratory services

- Physical and occupational therapy and speech-language pathology services

- Radiology and certain other imaging services

- Radiation therapy services and supplies

- Durable medical equipment and supplies

- Parenteral and enteral nutrients, equipment, and supplies

- Prosthetics, orthotics, and prosthetic devices and supplies

- Home health services

- Outpatient prescription drugs

- Inpatient and outpatient hospital services

There are important exceptions to the self-referral ban. A few most likely to affect ob-gyns include the following:

- A physician service you or another physician in your group performs or supervises

- In-office ancillary services

- Compensation paid to you by the provider to which you refer if the compensation is based on the fair market value of services you provide and is not affected by the volume or value of referrals you make

It is important to ensure that you comply with the Stark rules because violations can be expensive:

- Repayment of any payments received for illegal referrals

- Fines of up to $15,000 per violation

- Exclusion from the Medicare and Medicaid programs

The Stark regulations are complex and technical, so consult with a qualified attorney to evaluate financial relationships you have or are considering with other health care providers.

Medicare and Medicaid Coding and Billing Requirements

Making sure you follow Medicare and Medicaid billing requirements can be a challenge. Rules are numerous and change frequently. Helpful resources include:

- ACOG's coding education programs and materials (http://www.acog. org/from_home/departments/dept_web.cfm?recno=6)

- HHS Office of Inspector General's Compliance Program for Individual and Small Group Physician Practices (http://www.oig.hhs.gov/fraud/ complianceguidance.html)

Civil Rights Act

Your practice is subject to two federal laws intended to protect individuals against discrimination. One of these laws is the Civil Rights Act.

Title VI of the Civil Rights Act prohibits discrimination on the basis of national origin. If you receive federal financial assistance (for example, you participate in Medicare, Medicaid, or other federally funded programs), you must take reasonable steps to ensure that patients with limited English proficiency receive the language assistance necessary to provide "meaningful access" to your services. Language assistance services must be provided at no cost. The Department of Health and Human Services Office for Civil Rights has developed guidance for complying with the language assistance requirement. The guidance is available at http://www.hhs.gov/ocr/lep/.

Your obligations depend on several factors:

- The size of your practice

- The size of the patient population with limited English proficiency

- The nature of the services you provide

- How often you encounter particular languages

- How often patients with limited English proficiency come to your practice

Enforcement of the language assistance requirements is triggered by complaints:

- If the Office for Civil Rights receives a complaint that your practice is not complying with the requirements, it will investigate the complaint to find out whether you are in compliance.

- You will receive written notice of the steps you need to take to comply with the law.

- The Office for Civil Rights will provide technical assistance and resources to help you make corrections.

You cannot discriminate against job applicants or current employees on the basis of their disabilities.

If you do not take steps to comply voluntarily, you could be excluded from Medicare and Medicaid or the Office for Civil Rights could refer the case to the Department of Justice.

Note that while the requirement to provide language assistance technically applies only to recipients of federal financial assistance, it may not always be clear if you would be considered a beneficiary of federal financial assistance. It is not safe to assume, if your private practice does not accept Medicare or Medicaid patients, that you have no obligation to provide language assistance. Your relationship with a hospital that is a recipient of federal funds, for example, might trigger the requirement.

Americans With Disabilities Act

As stated, your practice is subject to two federal laws intended to protect individuals against discrimination; the second of these is the Americans With Disabilities Act (ADA). Because a physician's office is considered a public accommodation, your office must comply with ADA protections for people with disabilities. These protections apply both to employees and patients. The ADA defines disability to include physical and mental impairments that substantially limit one or more major life activities. If your practice employs 15 or more people, the following provisions apply:

- You cannot discriminate against job applicants or current employees on the basis of their disabilities.

- You must make reasonable accommodations for disabled employees (eg, modifying office equipment so a disabled employee can use it) unless the accommodations would impose an undue burden on the practice.

- You are not required to hire an unqualified job applicant with a disability, as long as your decision is based on objective criteria related to the job and the applicant could not carry out the job duties with reasonable accommodations.

You are also required to provide and pay for communication assistance needed by patients with disabilities that affect vision, speech, or hearing. Communication assistance could include the following:

- A sign language interpreter for an office visit with a hearing impaired patient

- Written materials and office notices in Braille or large print

- Assistive listening devices

You have some flexibility in providing communication assistance and are not required to make accommodations that impose an undue hardship. Be aware, however, that the fact that the cost of providing the accommodation might be higher than the payment for the service would not, in itself, be considered an undue hardship.

Additional information about the ADA is available from the Department of Justice (DOJ). Contact the DOJ at 800-514-0301 or www.usdoj.gov/crt/ada. Also see ACOG's *Guidelines for Women's Health Care* and *Special Issues in Women's Health Care*.

Occupational Safety and Health Administration Regulations

The Occupational Safety and Health Administration (OSHA) sets and enforces job safety and workplace health standards for all employers and employees and monitors job-related injuries and illnesses. The agency can conduct unannounced inspections of your office. If your practice does not comply with OSHA standards, you could be subject to civil or criminal penalties.

Physician offices may be most affected by OSHA's regulations on occupational exposure to bloodborne pathogens. The purpose of the regulations is to minimize transmission of human immunodeficiency virus (HIV), hepatitis B virus, and other infectious material in the workplace. The regulations cover employees in physician offices, hospitals, medical laboratories, and other health care facilities where workers could come into contact with blood or other potentially infectious material.

Your practice must develop an Exposure Control Plan to eliminate or minimize employees' exposure to bloodborne pathogens. The plan must include the following:

- Mandatory universal precautions for handling blood and other bodily fluids

- Engineering and work practice controls (eg, handwashing facilities and protocols, sharps disposal, equipment decontamination)

- Personal protective equipment provided to employees at no cost

- Housekeeping procedures

- Hepatitis B vaccination provided at no cost to employees at risk of workplace exposure

- Postexposure evaluation, follow-up, and documentation in the employee's medical record

- Communication of hazards to employees

- Employee training and documentation of the training

- Sharps injury log

You will need to review the plan each year, updating it to incorporate technological improvements that reduce exposure to bloodborne pathogens. See ACOG's *Guidelines for Women's Health Care* for a more in-depth discussion. Detailed information about the regulations for bloodborne pathogens is available from OSHA at the following case-sensitive address: http://www.osha.gov/SLTC/bloodborne pathogens/index.html.

Clinical Laboratory Improvement Amendments of 1988

The Clinical Laboratory Improvement Amendments of 1988 (CLIA) established federal oversight of all laboratory tests performed on humans (except for research). If you perform tests as simple as a urine dipstick in your office, you must comply with CLIA.

All laboratories, including those in physician offices, must apply to the Centers for Medicare and Medicaid Services (CMS) for a CLIA certificate. There are several categories of certificates, depending on the complexity of the tests performed. Most ob-gyn practices have either certificates of waiver or certificates for provider-performed microscopy procedures.

Certificate of Waiver

The Centers for Medicare and Medicaid Services has designated certain tests as "waived." If your office performs only waived tests according to manufacturers' instructions, apply for a certificate of waiver, which costs $150 and must be renewed every 2 years. A certificate of waiver will exempt you from many CLIA requirements, although CMS may conduct random announced or unannounced inspections of your office laboratory. A few examples of waived tests include the following:

- Urine pregnancy test by color comparison

- Fecal occult blood test

- Blood count spun microhematocrit

- Ovulation test by color comparison for human luteinizing hormone

Review the complete list of waived tests at http://www.cms.hhs.gov/clia/.

Certificate for Provider-Performed Microscopy Procedures

If physicians or mid-level practitioners in your office perform microscopy tests in addition to any waived tests, you must obtain a certificate for provider-performed microscopy procedures (PPMP). The PPMP certificate fee is $200 and must be renewed every 2 years. Requirements under a PPMP certificate are more stringent than those for waived tests only:

- Your practice must designate a laboratory director, either a physician or a mid-level practitioner licensed to practice independently in your state. If required by the state, the director must possess a current license as a laboratory director issued by the state in which the laboratory is located.

- A physician or a mid-level practitioner under physician supervision or practicing independently must perform all tests.

- You can perform tests only for your own or your practice's patients during the patient's visit.

- Your laboratory must comply with CLIA requirements for proficiency testing, patient test management, quality control, and quality assurance.

- The CMS may conduct announced or unannounced inspections.

A complete list of provider-performed microscopy procedures is available at http://www.cms.hhs.gov/clia/. Those that might be performed in ob-gyn offices include the following:

- Wet mounts, including preparations of vaginal, cervical, or skin specimens

- Postcoital direct, qualitative examinations of vaginal or cervical mucus

- Urinalysis, microscopic only

- Semen analysis presence and motility of sperm excluding Huhner

See ACOG's *Guidelines for Women's Health Care* to learn more about CLIA. Details about CLIA requirements and application procedures are available from your CMS Regional Office or CMS' CLIA website, http://www.cms.hhs.gov/clia/.

Federal government requirements that are meant to reduce fraud and abuse, increase access to care, and promote patient and employee safety affect your practice on a daily basis. This chapter has provided highlights of a number of federal government requirements relevant to ob-gyns. Your state probably also has statutes and regulations that affect the day-to-day operation of your practice. Full compliance with all government requirements that apply to your practice can be complex. Consult the resources listed in this chapter, as well as your state medical society and qualified legal and financial advisors, to ensure that your practice complies.

KEY POINTS

✓ Government requirements affect the organization and operation of your practice every day.

✓ Failing to comply can be costly.

✓ Consult experts knowledgeable about Stark and Antikickback requirements on issues related to financial agreements with other health providers.

✓ Contact government agencies for assistance in complying with the Americans With Disabilities Act, Health Insurance Portability and Accountability Act of 1996, and Civil Rights Act. They really are there to help.

Chapter 13

Physician Reporting Requirements and Profiling

As part of efforts to improve the availability of information about health care practitioners, the federal government and some states have established data banks for the reporting of information about actions taken against health care professionals, including physicians. This chapter will make you aware of some of these requirements, how they may affect you, and how you can learn more. The following are addressed in this chapter:

- National Practitioner Data Bank (NPDB)
- Healthcare Integrity and Protection Data Bank (HIPDB)
- State Physician Profiling

National Practitioner Data Bank

The Health Care Quality and Improvement Act of 1986 established the NPDB to create a central source of information about disciplinary actions taken against physicians, dentists, and other health care professionals, as well as information about medical professional liability judgments and settlements. The federal Department of Health and Human Services (DHHS) operates the databank.

Congress had two primary goals in setting up the NPDB:

- Encouraging state licensing boards, hospitals, other health care organizations, and professional societies to identify and punish health care providers who engage in unprofessional behavior
- Stopping "incompetent" health care professionals from moving from state to state without their history of disciplinary actions or medical liability cases following them

To achieve these goals, the NPDB requires hospitals and other health care organizations to query the NPDB when verifying the credentials of its providers. For example, when you apply for hospital privileges the hospital must check the NPDB to find out whether it has any reports about you. The hospital also must query the NPDB about you every 2 years.

Who Must Report to the NPDB?

The following types of organizations must file reports to the NPDB about individual practitioners:

- State medical and dental boards must report disciplinary actions related to professional competence or conduct, including revocation, suspension, or surrender of licenses, censure, reprimand, and probation.

When you apply for hospital privileges the hospital must check the NPDB to find out whether it has any reports about you. The hospital also must query the NPDB about you every 2 years.

- Hospital and other health care entities must report any action taken to restrict a physician's or dentist's clinical privileges for more than 30 days, including voluntary surrender or restriction of privileges while under investigation or in return for not being investigated.

- Professional societies of physicians and dentists must report adverse membership actions taken because of issues of professional competence or conduct.

- Medical professional liability insurers or other entities making payments to settle a written medical liability claim or judgment against an individual health professional must report those payments to the NPDB.

Who Has Access to the NPDB?

Access to the information in the NPDB is limited to:

- State licensing and disciplinary boards

- Hospitals and other health care organizations conducting peer review of members and prospective members of their medical staff and employees or potential employees

- Plaintiff's attorneys in medical liability suits against a hospital and physician when the hospital failed to check the NPDB about the named physician

- Individual health care professionals (limited to inquiries about themselves)

The Federal Privacy Act of 1974 protects the confidentiality of the information in the NPDB. The public cannot access the NPDB.

How Is the NPDB Related to Medical Professional Liability Claims?

If your medical professional liability carrier or another entity, such as a hospital, makes a payment on your behalf to settle or satisfy a judgment in a medical liability claim, that entity must make a report to the NPDB within 30 days:

- Payments made on behalf of licensed residents are included.

- Information must also be reported to the state medical licensing board in the state where the incident occurred.

- The definition of medical liability action includes any written complaint or demand for monetary compensation. (For example, a refund of your fee would be reportable if it resulted from a written demand for monetary damages and your insurer paid the refund.)

- Payments you make on your own behalf are not required to be reported.

- A lawsuit in which you were formally dropped before a settlement or judgment was reached does not have to be reported.

Each entity that makes a payment for the benefit of a practitioner in settlement of or in satisfaction in whole or in part of a claim or a judgment against the practitioner must report the payment information to the NPDB. Under the current rules, a payment made on behalf of an entity (hospital, clinic, or group practice) is not reportable. If a practitioner or other person makes a medical malpractice payment out of his or her personal funds, the payment is not reportable.

Your insurer will submit a standard Medical Malpractice Payment Report form reporting the following information:

- Physician name, home and work addresses, date of birth, professional schools attended, and hospital affiliations

- Date(s) of the alleged act(s)

- Jurisdiction where the claim was filed

- Date of judgment or settlement

- Amount and date of payment

In addition, the report will include a narrative description of 2,000 characters or less describing the incident and classifying the claim according to codes established by DHHS. The insurer making the payment writes this report. If you consider settling a case, the wording of the report should be a crucial issue in the settlement discussions:

- Discuss the wording of the narrative description before agreeing to a settlement.

- If the case is without medical merit and you are settling only because defending the case will be too costly, try to ensure that the description explicitly indicates this.

- Try to negotiate the wording in the report before the settlement. The 30-day deadline for filing the report provides limited time for negotiating the wording after the settlement is made.

The NPDB will notify you that it has received a report about a medical liability payment made on your behalf. After you receive the "Notification of a Report in the Data Bank(s)," you should:

- Review the report carefully and promptly.

- If there are errors, first contact your insurer or whoever made the payment and report and request that the errors be corrected.

- If your insurer does not correct the errors, file a formal dispute with the NPDB.

- Do not delay reviewing the report and requesting correction of errors; there is a time limit for filing a dispute.

Only health plans and federal or state government agencies can file reports to the HIPDB.

You also may append your own 2,000-character narrative statement to the report. Take special care in drafting this report. The NPDB will release your unedited statement along with the report in response to queries about you. Information about disputing an NPDB report, filing an appeal, and querying the databank is available from the NPDB Helpline (800-767-6732) or from the office NPDB web site (http://www.npdb-hipdb.hrsa.gov).

Putting the NPDB in Perspective

Although the existence of a national database of reports about physicians may be unsettling, do not be overly concerned about the NPDB. Do keep the NPDB reporting requirements in mind if you are thinking about settling a medical professional liability claim. Remember, though:

- Most credentialing bodies ask for more information than what is in an NPDB report.

- When your credentials are verified, typically you will have to report all open and closed medical liability claims, including those that were dropped or settled without payment.

- The NPDB includes only reports on closed claims with payments made on your behalf.

Healthcare Integrity and Protection Data Bank

The Health Insurance Portability and Accountability Act of 1996 created the HIPDB as a national health care fraud and abuse data collection program. The Department of Health and Human Services administers this database also. Congress developed the HIPDB as part of efforts to reduce the enormous financial burden imposed on the health care system by fraud and abuse. The HIPDB web site estimates that losses from health care fraud consume from 3% to 10% of all health care expenditures in the United States.

What Is the Purpose of the HIPDB?

The HIPDB helps federal and state agencies (including law enforcement agencies), state licensing boards, and health plans gather information about final adverse actions taken against health care practitioners, providers, or suppliers:

- HIPDB is a supplement to other sources of information, and is intended to be a flagging system to indicate that a more thorough review might be needed.

- Reports in the HIPDB should be considered in context with other information about a provider.

What Information Is in the HIPDB?

Only health plans and federal or state government agencies can file reports to the HIPDB. Types of information reported include the following:

- Licensure and certification actions

- Exclusion from participation in federal and state health care programs

- Criminal convictions in federal or state court related to health care

- Civil judgments in federal or state court related to health care

The HIPDB does *not* include:

- Settlements in which no findings or admissions of liability are made

- Medical professional liability claims

If you are the subject of a report to the HIPDB, you will receive a "Notification of a Report in the Data Bank(s)." If you receive this notification, act promptly:

- Review the report for accuracy.

- If necessary, file a dispute with the HIPDB.

- Add your own 2,000 character statement to the report if you wish.

Who Has Access to the HIPDB?

Access to the information in the HIPDB is limited to the following:

- State and federal government agencies

- Health plans

- Individual health care practitioners, providers, and suppliers (limited to information about themselves)

Additional information about the HIPDB, including instructions for submitting a self-query, is available at http://www.npdb-hipdb.hrsa.gov.

State Physician Profiling

In an effort to give patients information that may help them make better health care decisions, many states provide public access to "physician profiles." Information contained in these profiles varies widely and may include:

- Primary work setting and address

- Education and training

- State medical board disciplinary actions

- Revocation or restriction of hospital privileges

- Medical professional liability judgments and settled claims

- Criminal convictions

Some states provide Internet access to the profiles and others offer toll free telephone access. Learn how your state handles profiles:

- Find out whether your state releases physician profile information to the public. Start by checking with your state medical licensing board or health department.

- If your state does maintain profiles, check yours for accuracy and promptly correct any errors.

In addition to state profiling programs, the Federation of State Medical Boards sells a report on disciplinary actions against physicians.

KEY POINTS

✓ The National Practitioner Data Bank (NPDB) collects information about medical professional liability payments, clinical privilege restrictions, and disciplinary actions.

✓ Hospitals and health plans must check the NPDB for reports about individual physicians when verifying credentials.

✓ The Healthcare Integrity and Protection Data Bank (HIPDB) collects information about licensure and certification restrictions, criminal convictions related to health care, civil judgments related to health care, and exclusions from state and federal health care programs.

✓ The public does not have access to the NPDB or HIPDB.

✓ If you are settling a medical liability claim, pay close attention to the report that your insurer will file with the NPDB.

✓ If you are the subject of a report to the NPDB or HIPDB, be sure to review the report, request correction of errors, and consider appending your own statement.

✓ Review the information in any physician profiles your state may make available to the public.

Bibliography

American Academy of Pediatrics. Coping with malpractice litigation stress. In: Medical liability for Pediatricians. 6th ed. Elk Grove Village (IL): AAP; 2004. p. 187–92.

American Academy of Pediatrics, American College of Obstetricians and Gynecologists. Neonatal encephalopathy and cerebral palsy: defining the pathogenesis and pathophysiology. Elk Grove Village (IL): AAP; Washington, DC: ACOG; 2003.

American Academy of Pediatrics. Telephone care. In: Medical liability for pediatricians. 6th ed. Elk Grove Village (IL): AAP; 2004. p. 51–61.

American College of Emergency Physicians. On-call responsibilities for hospitals and physicians. Quality Advisory. Available at: http://www3.acep.org/practres.aspx?id=30122. Retrieved October 10, 2007.

American College of Obstetricians and Gynecologists. Access to reproductive health care for women with disabilities. In: Special issues in women's health. Washington, DC: ACOG; 2005. p. 39–59.

American College of Obstetricians and Gynecologists. Assisting hearing impaired and non-English speaking patients. Available at: http://www.acog.org/departments/dept_notice.cfm?recno=19&bulletin=1726. Retrieved October 10, 2007.

American College of Obstetricians and Gynecologists. Code of professional ethics of the American College of Obstetricians and Gynecologists. Washington, DC: ACOG; 2004. Available at: http://www.acog.org/from_home/acogcode.pdf. Retrieved October 16, 2007.

American College of Obstetricians and Gynecologists. Cultural competency, sensitivity, and awareness in the delivery of health care. In: Special issues in women's health. Washington, DC: ACOG; 2005. p. 11–20.

American College of Obstetricians and Gynecologists. Expert witness affirmation. Available at: http://www.acog.org/departments/download/ExpertWitnessAffirmation.pdf. Retrieved October 15, 2007.

American College of Obstetricians and Gynecologists. From exam room to courtroom: navigating litigation and coping with stress [CD-ROM]. Washington, DC: ACOG; 2006.

American College of Obstetricians and Gynecologists. Guidelines for women's health care. 3rd ed. Washington, DC: ACOG; 2007.

American College of Obstetricians and Gynecologists. HIPAA explained. Available at: http://www.acog.org/departments/dept_notice.cfm?recno=19&bulletin=1764. Retrieved October 15, 2007.

American College of Obstetricians and Gynecologists. Induction of labor. ACOG Practice Bulletin 10. Washington, DC: ACOG; 1999.

American College of Obstetricians and Gynecologists. Operative vaginal delivery. ACOG Practice Bulletin 17. Washington, DC: ACOG; 2000.

American College of Obstetricians and Gynecologists. Patient communication. In: Special issues in women's health. Washington, DC: ACOG; 2005. p. 3–9.

American College of Obstetricians and Gynecologists. Qualifications for the physician expert witness. Washington, DC: ACOG; 2003. Available at: http://www.acog.org/departments/download/ExpertWitnessQualifications.pdf. Retrieved October 15, 2007.

American College of Obstetricians and Gynecologists. Recognizing the need to speak the patient's language. at http://www.acog.org/departments/dept_notice.cfm?recno=19&bulletin=2150. Retrieved October 10, 2007.

American College of Obstetricians and Gynecologists. Stark II, phase 1: the self referral law. Available at: http://www.acog.org/departments/dept_notice.cfm?recno=19&bulletin=1788. Retrieved October 15, 2007.

American College of Obstetricians and Gynecologists. The assistant: information for improved risk management. Washington, DC: ACOG; 2001.

American College of Obstetricians and Gynecologists. The business of medicine: an essential guide for obstetrician–gynecologists. Washington, DC: ACOG; 2005.

American Medical Association. EMTALA quick reference guide for on-call physicians. Chicago (IL): AMA; 2003. Available at: http://www.ama-assn.org/ama1/pub/upload/mm/21/emtalarefguide.doc. Retrieved October 16, 2007.

American Medical Association. Guidelines for Physician-Patient Electronic Communications. Chicago (IL): AMA; 2004. Available at: http://www.ama-assn.org/ama/pub/category/print/2386.html. Retrieved October 16, 2007.

American Medical Association. Medicolegal forms with legal analysis: documenting issues in the patient-physician relationship. Chicago (IL): AMA; 1999.

Apfel D. Loss of chance in obstetrical cases. Trial 1993;29:48–55.

Center for Health Care Strategies, Inc. What is health literacy? Hamilton (NJ): CHCS; 2005. Available at: http://www.chcs.org/usr_doc/Health_Literacy_Fact_Sheets.pdf. Retrieved October 16, 2007.

Center for Health Care Strategies, Inc. Who has health literacy problems? Hamilton (NJ): CHCS; 2005. Available at: http://www.chcs.org/usr_doc/Health_Literacy_Fact_Sheets.pdf. Retrieved October 16, 2007.

Charles SC. Coping with a medical malpractice suit. West J Med 2001;174:55–8.

Charles SC. The stress of litigation: do we still have something to fear? Prim Care Update Ob Gyns 2003;10:60–5.

Coping with the stress of medical professional liability litigation. ACOG Committee Opinion No. 406. American College of Obstetricians and Gynecologists, May 2008.

Electronic fetal heart rate monitoring: research guidelines for interpretation. National Institute of Child Health and Human Development Research Planning Workshop. Am J Obstet Gynecol 1997;177:1385–90.

Expert testimony. ACOG Committee Opinion No. 374. American College of Obstetricians and Gynecologists. Obstet Gynecol 2007;110:445–6.

Federico F, Augello T. Disclosure from a risk manager's perspective. Forum 2003;23(2):10–2.

Federico F. Disclosure challenges and opportunities. Forum 2003;23(2):2–3.

Flory J, Emanuel E. Interventions to improve research participants' understanding in informed consent for research: a systematic review. JAMA 2004;292:1593–601.

Kachalia A, Studdert DM. Professional liability issues in graduate medical education. JAMA 2004;292:1051–6.

Kane B, Sands DZ. Guidelines for the clinical use of electronic mail with patients. The AMIA Internet Working Group, Task Force on Guidelines for the Use of Clinic-Patient Electronic Mail. J Am Med Inform Assoc 1998;5:104–11.

MAG Mutual. EMTALA – final rule: duties of on-call physicians. Atlanta (GA): MAG Mutual; 2003. Available at: http://www.magmutual.com/risk/EMTALA.html. Retrieved October 16, 2007.

Martin JA, Hamilton BE, Sutton PD, Ventura SJ, Menacker F, Kirmeyer S. Births: final data for 2004. Natl Vital Stat Rep 2006;55:1–101.

Medicare program; clarifying policies related to the responsibilities of Medicare-participating hospitals in treating individuals with emergency medical conditions. Final rule. Fed Regist 2003;68:53222–64.

National Association of Mutual Insurance Companies. Joint and several liability reform states. Available at: http://www.namic.org/reports/tortReform/JointAndSeveralLiability.asp. Retrieved October 16, 2007.

National Cancer Institute. Probability of breast cancer in American women. Bethesda (MD): NCI; 2006. Available at: http://www.cancer.gov/cancertopics/factsheet/Detection/probability-breast-cancer. Retrieved October 16, 2007.

National Institute of Child Health and Human Development, National Institute of Neurological and Communicative Disorders and Stroke. Prenatal and perinatal factors associated with brain disorders. NIH Publication No. 85-1149. Bethesda (MD): National Institutes of Health; 1985.

National Practitioner Data Bank, Healthcare Integrity and Protection Data Bank. Fact sheet on the Healthcare Integrity and Protection Data Bank. Chantilly (VA): NPDB; HIPDB; 2006. Available at: http://www.npdb-hipdb.hrsa.gov/pubs/fs/Fact_Sheet-Healthcare_Integrity_and_Protection_Data_Bank.pdf. Retrieved October 16, 2007.

National Practitioner Data Bank, Healthcare Integrity and Protection Data Bank. Fact sheet on the National Practitioner Data Bank. Chantilly (VA): NPDB; HIPDB; 2006. Available at: http://www.npdb-hipdb.hrsa.gov/pubs/fs/Fact_Sheet-Healthcare_Integrity_and_Protection_Data_Bank.pdf. Retrieved October 16, 2007.

Nora PF, editor. The psychological trauma of a medical malpractice suit: a practical guide. In: Professional liability/risk management: a manual for surgeons. Chicago (IL): American College of Surgeons; 1997. p. 235–51.

Offit K, Groeger E, Turner S, Wadsworth EA, Weiser MA. The "duty to warn" a patient's family members about hereditary disease risks. JAMA 2004;292:1469–73.

Oppenheim E. Loss-of-chance doctrine: the forgotten soldier in medical negligence litigation. Med Malpract Law Strategy 2001;18:5–8.

Physician Litigation Stress Resource Center. St. Joseph (MI): PLSRC; 2007. Available at: http://www.physicianlitigationstress.org. Retrieved November 28, 2007.

Popp P. Disclosing medical errors: how will it affect future litigation? Forum 2003;23:8–9.

Scroggs JA. Protecting assets – more than insurance. ACOG Clin Rev 2002;7(5):1, 8–10.

Staller JM. The "lost chance" theory of recovery: theory is gaining ground in future-harm claims. Med Malpract Law Strategy 2004;21(3):1–2, 4.

Strunk AL, Kenyon S. Medicolegal considerations in the diagnosis of breast cancer. Obstet Gynecol Clin North Am 2002;29:43–9.

United States Department of Health and Human Services, Office for Civil Rights. Guidance to federal financial assistance recipients regarding Title VI and the prohibition against national origin discrimination affecting limited English proficient persons—summary. Washington, DC: OCR; 2007. Available at: http://www.hhs.gov/ocr/lep/summaryguidance.html. Retrieved October 17, 2007.

United States Department of Health and Human Services, Office of Inspector General. Inspector General announces eight new anti-kickback statute safe harbors. Washington, DC: OIG; 1999. Available at: http://oig.hhs.gov/fraud/docs/safeharborregulations/safenr.htm. Retrieved October 17, 2007.

Vaginal birth after previous cesarean delivery. ACOG Practice Bulletin No. 54. American College of Obstetricians and Gynecologists. Obstet Gynecol 2004;104: 203–12.

Weathering malpractice litigation. OBG Manage 2000;12(5):88, 103–4.

Wilson N, Strunk AL. Overview of the 2006 ACOG Survey on Professional Liability. ACOG Clin Rev 2007;12(2):1, 13–6.

Glossary

ADA: See Americans With Disabilities Act

Abandonment: Termination of a physician–patient relationship without reasonable notice and without an opportunity for the patient to acquire adequate medical care, which results in some type of damage to the patient.

Admissibility (in Evidence): A characteristic of evidence that may properly be introduced in a legal proceeding. The determination as to admissibility is based on legal rules of evidence and is made by the trial judge or a screening panel.

Admissions: Statements by a party that are admissible in evidence as an exception to the hearsay rule. In a professional liability proceeding, an admission would typically be a statement of culpability by the defendant.

Admissions Against Interest: An out-of-court statement or admission of truth, usually by a party to a lawsuit, that when made is against that person's best interest or welfare. Such statements are admissible under an exception to the hearsay rule.

Affidavit: A voluntary, written statement of facts made under oath before an officer of the court or before a notary public. May be used at trial.

Affirmative Defense: An answer to a complaint that asserts a legal basis to excuse or foreclose liability (eg, expiration of statute of limitations, contributory negligence). *See also* Comparative Negligence/Contributory Negligence.

Allegation: A statement of a party to an action, made in a pleading, setting out what the party expects to prove.

Americans With Disabilities Act (ADA): Federal law that prohibits certain employers from discriminating against disabled persons when making decisions to hire, promote, or take other employment-related actions.

Answer: A legal document that contains a defendant's written response to a Complaint or Declaration in a legal proceeding. The Answer typically either denies the allegations of the plaintiff or makes new allegations as to why the plaintiff should not recover.

Appeal: The process by which a decision of a lower court is brought for review to a court of higher jurisdiction, typically known as an appellate court.

Appellate Court: The court that reviews trial court decisions. Appellate courts review the trial court proceedings and determine whether there were errors of law committed by the trial court. The appellate court does not make determinations respecting disputed questions of fact.

Arbitration: A method of dispute resolution in which a neutral third party (arbitrator) renders a decision after a hearing at which both parties are given the opportunity to present their cases. The decision can be binding or nonbinding depending on state law and/or the prior agreement of the parties.

Bailiff: An officer of the court who is in charge of courtroom decorum, directs witnesses to the witness stand, and attends to the jurors.

Battery: The unauthorized and offensive touching of a person by another. In medical professional liability cases, battery typically is contact of some type with a patient who has not consented to the contact. Battery can be either a civil or a criminal offense.

Bench Trial: A trial without a jury, wherein the judge determines the facts as well as the law. Also known as court trial or judge trial.

Borrowed Servant: One doctrine of vicarious liability in which an individual can be held liable for the negligent acts or omissions of another's employee if the employee is working under the individual's specific direction or control.

Burden of Proof: The necessity or duty of affirmatively proving a fact or facts in a dispute. The plaintiff typically has the burden of proof.

Captain-of-the-Ship: A doctrine whereby the physician in charge of a medical team is liable for the negligent acts of all members of the team. Historically applied most often to the team in an operating room, but not applied in most jurisdictions today.

Captive Insurance Company: A company owned and controlled by those it insures. For example, a hospital, hospital association, medical society, medical specialty society, or group of physicians that establishes its own medical professional liability insurance company.

Case: An action or cause of action; a matter in dispute; a lawsuit.

Case Law: Legal principles derived from judicial decisions. Case law differs from statutory law, which is enacted by legislatures.

Causation (or Cause): In negligence actions, a reasonable, proximate connection between a breach of duty and an injury sustained by the plaintiff.

Cause of Action: A set of alleged facts that a plaintiff uses to seek legal redress.

Claims-made Insurance Policy: A policy that covers only those claims that happen and are submitted during the term of the policy. Insurance coverage ceases on the date the policy is terminated unless extended reporting endorsement (tail) coverage is purchased. It is desirable that a claims-made policy include a guarantee for purchase of an extended reporting endorsement and waiver of premium for the extended reporting endorsement in the event of death, disability, or retirement (an insurance company's definition of retirement may vary).

Clerk of the Court: The person who is responsible for the administrative functions of the court. During a trial, the clerk administers the oaths to the witnesses, receives and marks exhibits into evidence, and requests the verdict from the jurors.

Clinical Laboratory Improvement Amendments (CLIA): Law established in 1988, which requires federal oversight for all laboratories, including physician offices, that perform tests on humans (except for research).

Collateral Source Rule: A rule of law that prevents a jury from considering and a court from subtracting any payments that the plaintiff has received from such sources as workmen's compensation, health insurance, government benefits, or sick pay benefits from the damage award.

Combining and Concurring Negligence: The legal doctrine under which one party can be held liable for an injury even if another party's negligence was a more important factor in causing the injury.

Commercial Insurance Company: A for-profit insurance company owned and controlled by stockholders (stock company) or policyholders (mutual company). Commercial or traditional insurance carriers are regulated by state law.

Common Law: That body of case law that was passed down to the American colonies by the British court system and has been interpreted and refined by judicial decisions (court decisions), as distinguished from statutory laws enacted by legislatures.

Comparative Negligence/Contributory Negligence: Affirmative defenses, one or the other of which is recognized in most jurisdictions.

- *Comparative Negligence:* An affirmative defense that compares the negligence of the defendant with that of the plaintiff. The plaintiff may recover damages from a negligent defendant even if the plaintiff and defendant are equally at fault. It is only when the plaintiff's negligence is greater than the defendant's that there can be no recovery. The plaintiff's damages are decreased, however, by the percentage that his or her own fault contributed to the overall damage.

- *Contributory Negligence:* An affirmative defense that prevents recovery against a defendant when the plaintiff's own negligence contributed to the injury, even though the defendant's negligence also may have contributed to the injury.

Complaint: A legal document that is the initial pleading on the part of the plaintiff in a civil lawsuit. A Complaint is sometimes known as a Declaration. The purpose of this document is to give a defendant notice of the alleged facts constituting the cause of action. The Complaint usually is attached to the Summons.

Compliance Program: A process designed to decrease or eliminate violations of federal requirements (eg, fraud and abuse, Americans With Disabilities Act,

Occupational Safety and Health Administration, Equal Employment Opportunity Commission).

Contingency Fee: A fee agreement between the plaintiff and the plaintiff's attorney, whereby the plaintiff agrees to pay the attorney a percentage of the damages recovered.

Counterclaim: A defendant's claim made in opposition to a claim made by the plaintiff (eg, malicious prosecution).

Court Reporter: A professionally trained stenographer who transcribes deposition or trial testimony.

Court Trial: A trial without a jury, wherein the judge determines the facts as well as the law; also known as bench trial or judge trial.

Culpability: Being at fault, deserving reproach or punishment for some act or course of action. Culpability connotes wrongdoing or errors of ignorance, omission, or negligence.

Damages: The sum of money a court or jury awards as compensation for a tort. The law recognizes certain categories of damages. These categories often are imprecise and inconsistent. Variations exist among jurisdictions, and all are not strictly adhered to by the courts. The major categories are general, punitive, exemplary, and special damages.

- *General Damages:* Typically intangible damages (eg, pain and suffering, disfigurement, interference with ordinary enjoyment of life).

- *Punitive or Exemplary Damages:* Damages awarded to the plaintiff to punish the defendant or act as a deterrent to others (eg, in cases of intentional tort or gross negligence).

- *Special Damages:* Out-of-pocket damages (eg, medical expenses, lost wages, rehabilitation).

Declaration: See Complaint.

Deductible: The amount of damages a physician must pay out-of-pocket before his or her professional liability insurer will pay. A deductible may apply to each claim or may apply for all damages within a policy year.

Defamation: An intentional false communication either published or publicly spoken, which injures a person's reputation or good name; this includes both libel and slander. Statements made in a court cannot be the basis for a defamation claim.

Defendant: The party against whom relief is sought in an action; in a criminal case, the accused.

Defensive Medicine: The practice of ordering unnecessary diagnostic tests and performing unnecessary services in order to strengthen a physician's defense against a possible future medical liability claim.

Deposition: A discovery procedure whereby each party may question in person the other party or anyone who may possibly be a witness. Depositions are conducted before the trial under oath and are admissible at trial under certain circumstances.

Directed Verdict: Ruling by the trial judge that, as a matter of law, the verdict must be in favor of a particular party. A verdict usually is directed because of a clear failure to meet the burden of proof, sometimes referred to as a failure to establish a prima facie case.

Discovery: Pretrial procedures to learn of evidence to minimize the element of surprise at the trial. These typically include Interrogatories and Depositions but also can include Requests for Admission of Facts and Requests for Genuineness of Documents.

Dismissal: A final disposition of an action, suit, motion, etc. To dismiss a motion is to deny it; to dismiss an appeal is to affirm the judgment of the trial court.

Due Care: The level of observation, awareness, and care owed by a physician to a patient.

Due Process: Legal procedures that have been established in systems or jurisprudence for the enforcement and protection of private rights. It often means simply a fair hearing or trial.

Duty: An obligation recognized by the law. A physician's duty to a patient is to provide the degree of care ordinarily exercised by physicians of the same or similar specialty practicing in the same community, or, increasingly, in the same country.

Emergency Medical Treatment and Active Labor Act (EMTALA): Federal law that ensures that everyone who seeks medical help from a hospital emergency department receives appropriate screening and treatment, regardless of the ability to pay.

Evidence: Facts presented at trial through witnesses, records, documents, and concrete objects, for the purpose of proving or defending a case. Some examples of evidence are:

- *Circumstantial Evidence:* Facts or circumstances that indirectly imply that the principal facts at issue actually occurred.

- *Demonstrative or Real Evidence:* The use of articles or objects rather than the statement of witnesses to prove a fact in question.

- *Direct Evidence:* Evidence that is based on personal knowledge or observation and that, if true, proves a fact without inference or presumption.

- *Material Evidence:* Evidence having some logical connection with the consequential facts.

- *Opinion Evidence:* Testimony of an expert witness based on special training or background, rather than on personal knowledge of the facts in issue.

- *Prima Facie Evidence:* A level of proof that is sufficient to establish a fact and, if not rebuffed, becomes conclusive of the fact.

Expert Opinion: The testimony of a person who has special training, knowledge, skill, or experience in an area relevant to resolution of the legal dispute.

Expert Witness: A person recognized by the court as a specialist in the subject matter of a trial who is permitted to present his or her opinion about the facts of the case without having been a witness to any of the events.

Extended Reporting Endorsement (Tail): A supplement or endorsement to a claims-made policy that provides coverage for any incident that occurred during the term of the claims-made policy but had not been brought as a claim by the time the insurer–policyholder relationship terminated. Tail coverage is purchased from a physician's existing carrier on termination or cancellation, and typically also is provided by the carrier on the physician's death, disability, or retirement.

Federal Court: Federal courts are another system of trial and appellate courts like state courts. However, federal courts accept only certain types of cases. Medical professional liability cases generally are not filed in the federal courts unless a patient is from one state and the health care practitioner is from another state.

Fiduciary: Having a special relationship to another that imposes legal duties to act responsibly and in good faith to protect that party's interests.

Fraud: An intentional misrepresentation of the truth or concealment of fact. Examples in medicine would be to exaggerate one's professional credentials to induce a patient to undergo tests or procedures or to misstate (upcode) diagnoses or treatment codes to maximize reimbursement.

Good Samaritan Statute: State laws enacted to encourage physicians, and others, to aid emergency victims. Statutes vary from state to state but generally grant immunity from liability for negligence when a caregiver acts gratuitously at the scene of an emergency and provides care in good faith. Because good Samaritan laws are state-specific, physicians are urged to familiarize themselves with the law in effect in their jurisdiction. Good Samaritan laws do not, in general, provide immunity to physicians who render assistance to other physicians or staff in hospitals.

Guaranty Fund: Established by law in every state, these funds usually are maintained by a state's insurance commission to protect policyholders in the event that a licensed insurer becomes insolvent or otherwise unable to meet its financial obligations. The funds usually are financed by assessments against all property and casualty insurers regulated by a state.

HIPAA: *See* Health Insurance Portability and Accountability Act of 1996.

Hammer Clause: A contractual provision that obligates the insured physician to pay damages in excess of a settlement amount recommended by the insurer if the physician rejects the recommended settlement and proceeds to trial.

Health Insurance Portability and Accountability Act of 1996 (HIPAA): The law is intended to ensure that persons have the opportunity to keep their insurance when they leave a job, and ensure that persons with preexisting conditions, such as pregnancy, are not denied insurance coverage. There are also three distinct sets of HIPAA regulations, finalized in 2001, that affect how a medical practice operates: 1) transaction and code sets, 2) security, and 3) privacy. The transaction and code set regulations require that health plans and providers use certain code sets, including *International Classification of Diseases, Ninth Revision, Clinical Modification* (ICD-9-CM) and *Current Procedural Terminology* (CPT).

Health Literacy: The ability to read, understand, and act upon appointment notices, medication, and self-care instruction, patient education materials, and consent forms.

Hearsay: An out-of-court statement, made by another person, offered in court to prove the truth of the facts contained in the statement. Hearsay generally is not admissible. There are, however, exceptions to the hearsay rule, such as an admission against interest.

Hostile Witness: A witness whose position or viewpoint is in opposition to that of the attorney who called him or her to the stand.

Hung Jury: A jury that cannot come to a decision that constitutes a verdict in its jurisdiction, frequently after lengthy deliberation. A hung jury results in a mistrial, which in most circumstances means the case will be retried before a new jury. *See also* Mistrial.

Hypothetical Question: A question that solicits the opinion of an expert witness at a trial or deposition based on a combination of assumptions and facts already introduced in evidence.

Impeachment: An attack on the credibility of a witness.

Informed Consent: A legal doctrine that requires a physician to obtain consent for treatment to be rendered or an operation to be performed; without an informed consent, the physician may be held liable for violation of the patient's rights, whether or not the treatment was appropriate and rendered with due care (*see* Battery).

Injunction: A court order prohibiting a party to do or continue to do a particular act.

Interrogatories: A discovery procedure in which one party submits a series of written questions to the opposing party, who must answer in writing under oath within a certain period. The answers are admissible at trial under certain circumstances.

JUA: See Joint Underwriting Association.

Joint and Several Liability: A legal doctrine whereby each individual defendant is independently responsible for the entire amount of damages awarded against all defendants.

Joint Underwriting Association (JUA): A state-sponsored insurance company that has been created to make insurance available in tight market conditions. A JUA may or may not be required to provide professional liability insurance to all licensed physicians in the state, depending on state law. The solvency of the JUA typically is supported by assessments on insurance carriers licensed to do business in the state.

Judge Trial: A trial without a jury, wherein the judge determines the facts as well as the law (also known as court trial or bench trial).

Judgment: The official decision in the record of a case, which is binding on the parties unless it is overturned or modified on appeal. A judgment typically consists of a finding in favor of one or more of the parties and an assessment of damages and costs.

Jury Trial: A trial in which 12 or fewer registered voters are impaneled to hear the evidence, determine the facts, and render a verdict. In most states, the verdict must be unanimous. Many states now empanel only six jurors and one or two alternates for civil, rather than criminal, cases.

Liability Limits: The maximum sum or sums that an insurance company is obligated to pay for a settlement or judgment against an insured party. In medical professional liability insurance policies, these limits generally are written with a limit per claim and a limit of aggregate liability for each year of coverage.

Libel: A false and malicious publication that injures the reputation of another.

Litigation: The process of a court trial to determine legal issues.

Loss of Chance: A legal theory that allows the plaintiff to argue that the physician's negligence reduced or eliminated her chance of survival or recovery. Under some interpretations, the loss of chance theory can allow patients to sue when chances of recovery or survival were significantly less than 51%.

Loss of Consortium: A claim for damages by the parent, child, or spouse of an injured party for the loss of care, comfort, society, and, when applicable, interference with sexual relations.

Maloccurrence: A bad medical outcome that is totally unrelated to the quality of care provided, ie, nonnegligent.

Malpractice: Professional negligence. In medical terms, it is the failure to exercise that degree of care used by reasonably careful physicians of like qualifications in the same or similar circumstances. The failure to meet this acceptable standard of care must cause the patient injury.

Mistrial: An action taken by a court, which terminates a trial in progress. A mistrial may be a result of some procedural error or serious misconduct during the proceedings, or a jury's inability to agree on a verdict.

Motion: Written or oral court plea requesting that a court or judge make an order or ruling affecting the lawsuit.

Negligence: Legal cause of action involving the failure to exercise due care expected of a reasonable person under the same or similar circumstances.

Nose Coverage: See Prior Acts.

Occupational Safety and Health Administration (OSHA): Entity responsible for developing and implementing job safety and health standards and regulations, which apply to all employers and employees.

Occurrence Insurance Policy: An insurance policy that obligates the insurer to pay for claims that took place during the period covered by the policy, regardless of when the claim is filed. This type of policy does not require that the policyholder purchase an extended reporting endorsement (tail) on termination.

PRO: See Peer Review Organization

Party: A person or legal entity involved in a legal transaction or court proceeding (eg, a party to the contract or a party to the lawsuit).

Peer Review Organization (PRO): A government agency or an independent joint contract with a private group to review medical necessity, quality of care, or cost issues for Medicare and Medicaid patients, generally in connection with observation or inpatient hospital care or both.

Periodic Payments: Damages paid to a plaintiff over a period of time instead of in a lump sum. If permitted by state law, periodic payments may be ordered when the damages exceed a certain amount.

Physician-owned Insurance Company: A company typically owned and controlled by physicians, but not required to be a nonprofit corporation. It may be a captive insurance company. In the past, such companies have sometimes been referred to as "bedpan mutuals."

Plaintiff: A party who initiates a lawsuit by filing a complaint with a clerk of the court against the defendant(s) demanding damages. In medical liability claims, typically the patient, family, or estate.

Pleadings: Written documents filed in a lawsuit, through which the issues in dispute are identified and clarified, including the plaintiff's cause of action and the defendant's grounds of defense. Pleadings include the Complaint, Answer, and Motions.

Preponderance of Evidence: The greater weight of evidence, or evidence that is more credible or convincing to the mind.

Prima Facie Case: A plaintiff's case with sufficient evidence to survive a motion for a directed verdict or a motion to dismiss by the defendant.

Prior Acts (Nose): A supplement or endorsement to a claims-made insurance policy that may be purchased from a new carrier when a physician changes carriers and previously had a claims-made insurance policy. A prior acts policy covers incidents that happened before the beginning of the new insurance relationship but that have yet to be reported or a claim brought forward. Prior acts can be an alternative to an extended reporting endorsement (tail).

Privileged Communications: Confidential communication between individuals that attains a special legal status because of the nature of their relationship. Privileged communications include communications between attorney and client, husband and wife, physician and patient, and priest and penitent.

Proportional Liability: A legal theory that allocates responsibility for damages to multiple defendants based on their relative share of blame for the injury.

Proximate Cause: An act or omission that, unbroken by any intervening cause, produces an injury. In a medical professional liability case, failure to adhere to the standard of care must be the proximate cause of the injury to the patient.

RPG: *See* Risk Purchasing Group

RRG: *See* Risk Retention Group

Rebut: Refute; present opposing evidence or arguments.

Reinsurance: Insurance purchased by a primary insurance carrier to reimburse it for settlements and judgments in excess of a specified limit.

Res Ipsa Loquitur: "The thing speaks for itself." A doctrine under which it can be demonstrated that the injury was caused by means under the defendant's exclusive control and would not have occurred in the absence of negligence. In medical professional liability cases, it allows a patient to prove his or her case without the necessity of an expert witness to testify that the defendant physician violated the standards of care. It is applicable only in those instances in which negligence is clear and obvious even to a layman, such as cases in which a surgeon leaves a sponge or other foreign object in the patient following surgery.

Reservation of Rights: An insurance term that refers to a carrier's conditional commitment to undertake the defense of a matter when there is a question as to the existence of coverage or the amount of coverage for an incident.

Respondeat Superior: "Let the master answer." The legal principle that makes an employer liable for civil wrongs committed by employees within the course and scope of their employment. In medical professional liability cases, this theory often is used to hold hospitals liable for the negligence of the staff employees and attending physicians responsible for residents.

Right to Consent to Settlement: A contractual provision in a professional liability insurance policy ensuring that the insurer cannot settle a claim without the insured physician's consent.

Risk Management: Activities and strategies aimed at improving medical care while decreasing exposure to professional liability and financial loss.

Risk Purchasing Group (RPG): A group of people or entities with similar liability risks that are permitted under federal law to organize across state lines to buy insurance. The carrier that sells insurance to the group must be licensed in at least one state but need not be licensed in every state where a member of the group resides. The purchasing group itself does not have to be licensed in any state and thus is neither subject to financial examination by state insurance departments nor covered by a state's guaranty fund.

Risk Retention Group (RRG): A special insurance entity that is limited to individuals or organizations engaged in similar activities with similar or related liability exposures; members must share a common business, trade, or profession. An RRG is required to comply with state insurance laws only in its state of incorporation. Once a group is licensed in one state, it can then sell insurance nationwide without fulfilling each state's licensure requirements. An RRG is allowed to contribute to a state's guaranty fund.

Self-insured or Self-funded Plan: A trust fund established to pay defense costs and liability losses on behalf of participants, typically established by a hospital, hospital association, or hospital corporation.

Settlement: An agreement made between the parties to a lawsuit or a claim, which resolves their legal dispute.

Slander: The speaking of false and malicious words that damage the reputation of another.

Standard of Care: A term used in the legal definition of medical professional liability. A physician is required to adhere to the standards of practice of competent physicians, with comparable training and experience, in the same or similar circumstances.

Stark I: Statute and regulations prohibiting a physician from referring a Medicare patient to a clinical laboratory in which the physician or an immediate family member has a financial interest (also known as the "physician self-referral ban").

Stark II: Third phase of the Stark law and regulations that extends the prohibition on physician self-referral to 10 additional designated health services and applies some aspects of the ban to the Medicaid program.

Statute of Limitations: The period in which a plaintiff may file a lawsuit. Once this period expires, the plaintiff's lawsuit is barred if the defendant asserts the affirmative defense of the statute of limitations. In medical liability cases, courts have adopted a variety of rationales to extend the period in which the plantiff may file a lawsuit, beyond the statutorily prescribed interval.

Stipulation: An agreement made by both parties to the litigation regulating any matter related to the case, proceeding, or trial. For instance, litigants can agree to extend the period for pleadings, admit certain facts into evidence at trial, or accept the authenticity of a hospital or other medical record.

Structured Settlement: Settlement agreement between the parties to a lawsuit or a claim in which the damages are paid to the plaintiff over a period of time, instead of in a lump sum. These settlements usually are financed through the purchase of an annuity.

Subpoena: Court order requiring a witness to appear at a certain proceeding to give testimony or produce documents or both.

Summary Judgment: Granting of a judgment in favor of either party before trial. Summary judgment is granted only when there is no factual dispute and one of the parties is entitled to judgment as a matter of law.

Summons: A legal document that is attached to the Complaint or Declaration in a lawsuit. It orders the defendant or the defendant's attorney to file an Answer within a specified period.

Tail Coverage: See Extended Reporting Endorsement

Tort: A civil wrong, for which an action can be filed in court to recover damages for personal injury or property damage resulting from negligent acts or intentional misconduct. To litigate a tort claim successfully, four elements must be established: 1) a duty owed; 2) a breach of that duty; 3) an injury caused by the breach; and 4) damages.

Trier of Fact: The jury or, in the case of trial without jury, the judge.

Underwriting: The selection process by which an insurance company evaluates the risk of loss and determines which of the risks (applicants) should be accepted. On an individual basis, underwriting also would determine the amounts and limits of coverage for individual applicants.

Utilization Review or Utilization Management: A technique or program that evaluates the appropriateness, quality, and medical necessity of services provided to plan members. It can be administered by the hospital, health maintenance organizations, or insurance carriers and can involve precertification of procedures and admissions, concurrent inpatient review, or retrospective review of patient medical records.

Verdict: The formal decision or finding made by a jury or judge. The verdict is in favor of the plaintiff or defendant, and damages usually are awarded when the verdict is in favor of the plaintiff.

Vicarious Liability: Civil liability for the actions of others. Physicians may be vicariously liable for the negligent acts of their employees committed within the scope of their employment (*see* Respondeat Superior). In the hospital setting, although relatively uncommon, a surgeon may be vicariously liable for the negligent acts of all members of the surgical team (*see* Captain-of-the-Ship).

Wanton Act: An act that shows reckless lack of concern for the safety or rights of another; more than negligence or gross negligence.

Work Product: Materials prepared by or for an attorney in anticipation of litigation. These materials are not subject to discovery.

Wrongful Birth: An action brought by parents who seek damages after the birth of an impaired child. The parents assert that they received inadequate medical care that led to the birth of a handicapped child or that if they had received proper genetic counseling or testing, the child's birth could have been avoided.

Wrongful Conception/Wrongful Pregnancy: An action brought by parents who seek damages for a healthy but unplanned and unwanted child born as a result of failed sterilization, birth control, or abortion.

Wrongful Life: An action brought by an impaired child who contends that if his or her parents had been correctly counseled about likely birth defects, he or she would have never been conceived or would have been aborted.

Appendixes

A. What To Do If You Are Sued

B. Qualifications for the Physician Expert Witness

C. Expert Witness Affirmation

D. Code of Professional Ethics of the American College of Obstetricians and Gynecologists

E. Professional Liability and Risk Management Check-up

Appendix A

What To Do If You Are Sued

Introduction

It's hard to believe it could happen, but one day you might receive a letter from a patient's attorney requesting a copy of the patient's medical records. It hits you—you are about to be sued. You wouldn't be alone.

Under the current liability system, the number of medical liability claims being filed against all physicians has climbed steadily in recent years. Obstetrician–gynecologists, with an average of 2.6 claims in a career span, are among the most frequently sued medical specialists. If a liability lawsuit does result in a verdict against the defendant physician, the damages award is often exorbitantly high, motivating the attorneys to search for more claims. It is only a matter of time before most ob-gyns experience a liability claim.

The American College of Obstetricians and Gynecologists (ACOG) recognizes the symptoms of another liability crisis. The College has joined in federal and state efforts to treat the system that is in critical condition. Meaningful reform is needed in our tort system and court procedures. Until such reform occurs, however, all of us must be prepared to practice within the realities of the current system.

This guide was developed to demystify the liability litigation process and to give you a quick summary of the various stages of medical liability litigation. We hope you will never have to use it, but if you do find yourself involved in medical liability litigation, consider each section a resource as you work your way through your case. The topics covered can serve as a basis for communication with your attorney and insurance carrier. We know that litigation is an unpleasant and often traumatic experience for physicians. By becoming an informed participant in the process, you will be better prepared to survive the ordeal.

Incident Management

An incident is an event that suggests the possibility of a medical liability lawsuit. Your appropriate management of an incident is of the utmost importance. A delay in reporting a suspected problem could make it difficult to prepare a successful defense.

Your first reactions to an incident can be critical to the outcome of a potential or actual lawsuit. You need to know what requirements and obligations your professional liability policy places on you. You will usually be required to notify your carrier as soon as a claim is made or suspected. Early notification, even as early as the occurrence itself, aids in early evaluation and preparation of a case, which, in turn, improves the chances of a successful defense should an actual claim develop. Such action affords the insurance company the opportunity to begin collecting and recording facts and evaluating the case for merit right away.

Signs of a Potential Lawsuit

There are several signs that a lawsuit is impending:

- *Complication:* An unexpected outcome during the treatment of your patient.

- *Dissatisfaction:* Direct complaints or expressions of dissatisfaction with an outcome from the patient or the patient's family.

- *Contact from an attorney:* A request from an attorney for information on a patient's treatment.

- *Request for medical records:* A written or verbal request for medical records by an attorney, another physician, or the patient herself.

  —Obtain written authorization from the patient before you release any information.

  —Send copies of the requested records and retain the originals for your files.

  —Keep a list of all records provided, those to whom they were sent, and the dates sent.

- *Noncompliance:* Your patient refuses a medical test/procedure or even hospitalization. Note your informed consent discussion in the patient's file. You might even want the patient to sign a form indicating her refusal of the specific treatment.

- *Failure to keep scheduled follow-up visits:* A patient misses a follow-up appointment. Document your efforts to contact the patient.

- *Dissatisfaction:* A patient who fails to pay a bill or unnecessarily delays payment could be dissatisfied and contemplating a lawsuit. You might assuage such patients with personal inquiries reflecting your concern with their satisfaction and possibly offer to establish a payment schedule if that would assist them.

Responding to an Incident

When an incident occurs that could lead to a lawsuit, the following actions are recommended:

- *Provide honest explanations and express empathy:* Sometimes the simplest of acts in response to an incident can help avoid a lawsuit. Some experts recommend that you honestly explain what happened to the patient and her family and express empathy. Don't avoid contact with the patient or her family at this stage. You would not want to be perceived as having something to hide. This is an extremely important point in patient care and risk management.

- *Notify insurance carrier:* Notify your insurance carrier about an unexpected outcome. Again, this will give you a head start in the event of litigation.

- *Review patient's records:* Be very familiar with the details of the specific case.

- *Keep attorney informed:* Any written or recorded information given to your insurance company is not privileged and is subject to discovery. Direct all communication related to the claim to your defense attorney once one has been assigned to your case, because information given to your attorney is protected by the attorney–client privilege.

- *Use caution in communications:* If a formal claim has been filed, you should not attempt to negotiate directly with the patient or her attorney because it could prejudice your position should a lawsuit follow. Make contemporaneous written notes of all oral communications with the patient or her family. Save any correspondence in a file separate from the patient's medical records.

Claims Management

A lawsuit begins when the plaintiff files a formal Complaint or Declaration, a legal document consisting of allegations and the legal basis to support a claim of professional medical liability against the defendant, requesting damages or other relief. Once a Complaint or Declaration has been filed, the court serves each defendant with a Summons. The Summons is usually attached to the Complaint or Declaration and requires the defendant to file a response, usually known as an Answer, within a specified period of time.

Your defense attorney will prepare the Answer and must respond to each of the allegations and issues. Failure to file an Answer may result in a default judgment against you. Failure to respond to allegations or issues may be considered as an admission of culpability. This matter deserves immediate attention; there are stringent penalties for not responding.

Responding to a Formal Claim

Appropriate responses to a formal claim include the following:

- *Notify your professional liability insurance company:* Immediately notify your insurer so that you and your attorney can appropriately respond to the Complaint or Declaration. Your insurance company will usually tell you the name of the attorney and the law firm assigned to your defense immediately after the lawsuit has been filed, if not before.

- *Deliver the Summons:* Send the Summons (including the attached Complaint or Declaration) to your defense attorney and/or your insurance carrier. Keep a copy for your records.

- *Prepare a case analysis for the attorney:* This could include a detailed, complete evaluation of the patient's medical files, such as all records, correspondence, X-rays, results of laboratory tests, and chronologic documentation of the medical data. Keep all of this information in a separate file. Materials that you prepare at the request of your attorney in preparation for litigation are not subject to discovery by the plaintiff's counsel because they are considered attorney work product.

- *Do not alter medical records:* You must not alter the medical records in any way. Evidence of tampering with the records can lead to a loss of credibility in court as well as a substantial increase in the size of an award. Tampering can render a case indefensible.

- *Never send originals:* Never send originals of requested records, only photocopies of requested records. Check with your attorney and be certain to have proper authorization from your patient.

- *Serve as a medical educational resource:* Review textbooks and medical articles related to the medical issues in the case and conduct MEDLINE searches, if possible. Educate your defense team about the strengths and weaknesses of the medical aspects of your case. It is important that your attorneys know about conflicting viewpoints and alternative treatments.

- *Be honest and open with your attorney:* Being caught off guard during a trial is the worst nightmare of a defense attorney.

- *Stay calm:* Your first reactions to a Summons might be surprise, anger, panic, and self-doubt. Try not to internalize this or take it personally; the majority of ob-gyns will be sued at some point in their career. Most important, it is unproductive to overreact or be hostile. There is much to do, and being level-headed is essential in preparing a successful defense.

Working With Your Defense Attorney

It is important to meet with the attorney assigned to your case as early as possible. Call to arrange an appointment as soon as you know who is assigned. It is vital to the outcome of your case that you feel comfortable and have a good rapport with your attorney. Therefore, consider your first meeting an evaluation period. If you encounter any problem that cannot be resolved, get in touch with your insurance carrier and request new counsel. Most carriers will respect your wishes and try to accommodate you. Never be afraid to ask your carrier questions if you have any reservations concerning your attorney.

Evaluating Your Attorney

Consider the following when evaluating your assigned attorney:

- Is your attorney competent?

  —Does he or she understand the medicine involved, or is he or she willing to learn?

  —Has he or she handled malpractice cases of this nature before?

  —What is the reputation of your attorney and of his or her firm? If you have questions, ask your personal attorney to inquire.

- Will your attorney personally handle the important aspects of your case?

  —Will he or she personally handle your deposition, the opposing expert's deposition, and the actual trial?

  —What will be the role of his or her associates in your defense?

- Does your attorney have a defense plan?

  —Will he or she include you sufficiently in preparation of the defense, ie, will you be looked to as a medical resource?

  —Will he or she devote adequate time to preparing the case, eg, deposition preparation, trial testimony preparation? What is his or her current caseload?

- Do you communicate well and feel comfortable with each other?

- Is there a conflict of interest?

  —Is he or she defending other codefendants and, if so, is there an actual or potential conflict between your position and that of any codefendant?

- Is your attorney more interested in the insurance carrier's interests than in yours?

  —Has he or she fully explained to you his or her obligations to you and the insurance carrier?

- Is your attorney's representation sufficient?

  —Have you been sued for more than the amount of your coverage?

  —Is your carrier defending you under a "reservation of rights," ie, your carrier questions whether there is coverage for the liability incident?

  —In a case of insufficient representation, retain personal defense counsel to protect your individual financial exposure. Although your personal defense counsel may not lead the defense, he or she will be working exclusively for you. In case of other problems, you are free to contact your insurance carrier and request new counsel.

Responsibilities of a Defendant Physician

As a defendant, you have certain responsibilities:

- As soon as an attorney is assigned, call to set up an initial appointment.
- Cooperate and participate in your defense.
  - —Learn the legal process.
  - —Listen well; your attorney is the expert on litigation procedures.
  - —Litigation is a time-consuming process; be prepared to set aside time for your attorney.
- Provide medical input.
  - —Participate in preparing your medical defense.
  - —Be sure your attorney is knowledgeable about medical facts.
  - —Research and provide medical literature relevant to the case.
  - —Educate your attorney in medical procedures.
- Provide a written chronologic summary of the incident.
- Explain your treatment rationale to your attorney.
  - —Review alternative treatments.
  - —Review medical strengths and weaknesses of the case.
- Review your personal documentation file on the incident with your attorney.
- Review with your attorney the possible need for visual aids and exhibits, and provide assistance in obtaining them.
- Act as a resource in identifying noted experts, when requested.
- Never withhold any pertinent information from your attorney.
  - —Regard yourself as the "patient;" your attorney needs a complete history.
  - —Be candid. Don't fail to give your attorney relevant information that could be more damaging if it was realized later.
  - —Don't be shy; ask questions and clear up any misunderstanding.
- Assist with the jury selection, if asked.

Responsibilities of Your Defense Attorney

Your attorney should:

- Keep you informed about litigation procedures
- Explain the significance of each stage of the proceedings
- Thoroughly prepare you for your role in the proceedings

- Carefully investigate and prepare the case by deciding strategy and tactics to defend you
- Evaluate all the factors that could win or lose the case for the defense:
  —The status of the medical records

  —The gravity of the injury and potential loss

  —The appearance and credibility of the plaintiff, the defendant, and the expert witnesses

  —The ability and experience of the plaintiff's attorney

  —The trial judge assigned to the case

  —The locale in which the case is to be tried

  —The caliber of the jurors

  —The outcome of similar cases in your jurisdiction
- Advise you on your court appearance and manner, including the importance of dress, demeanor, and communication skills

Frequent communication between you and your attorney is essential. It is important that you have a close and comfortable relationship in which neither of you is reluctant to speak out. Your attorney must be completely knowledgeable about the case, and you must be satisfied with his or her approach to your defense.

Settlement

Whether to settle will be an issue from the time an incident occurs through a final verdict, and perhaps beyond. Although settlement is not usually a formal part of pretrial or trial procedures, many more cases are settled than are contested to a conclusion. You should be aware of what a settlement is, when it can be used, and what your rights are. Your contract with your insurance carrier will indicate whether your insurer and your defense attorney can agree to settle without your consent.

A settlement is an agreement made between parties to an incident, claim, or lawsuit that resolves their legal dispute. A settlement is a financial disposition of a case without a decision on the merits. In most instances, payment is made to the plaintiff in exchange for a release, a legal document that absolves the defendant from all past, present, and future liability in connection with the incident. Most releases specifically state that the settlement by the defendant is not an admission of fault.

Any settlement of the case that results in a payment on your behalf must be reported to the National Practitioner Data Bank.

Who Wants to Settle and Why?

There are substantial costs and risks involved in litigating a case to a conclusion. The longer a case lasts, the more time, effort, and money are expended.

Each of the participants in the litigation process has reasons for preferring settlement:

- Judge
  - Wants to clear the calendar and dispose of cases quickly (To foster settlement, the judge may require the parties to participate in a pretrial settlement conference.)
- Insurance carrier
  - Limits defense costs
  - Establishes a fixed sum for payment
  - Avoids an uncertain jury verdict
- Plaintiff's attorney
  - Considers a settlement a victory
  - Ensures compensation to the client
  - Ensures compensation for time and effort
- Plaintiff
  - Ensures compensation
  - Avoids further delay
- Defense attorney
  - Avoids an uncertain jury verdict
- Defendant physician
  - Avoids an uncertain jury verdict
  - Avoids the potential of the verdict exceeding his or her insurance coverage
  - Eliminates further commitment of time and energy to the litigation process

What Factors May Influence the Decision of Whether to Settle?

During the course of any discussion regarding settlement, myriad factors may come into play:

- Evidence
  - Missing medical records or unavailable witnesses
  - Illegible or altered records
- Expert witnesses
  - Lack of expert support for the plaintiff or the defense
  - Quality of expert opinion for the plaintiff or the defense

- Previous decision of a review committee or panel, if any, and whether that decision is admissible in evidence at trial
- Amount of damages being asked by the plaintiff
  —Seriousness of injuries
  —Influence of the "sympathy factor" on a jury
- Verdict potential
  —The estimated amount or the plaintiff's demand exceeds the limits of insurance coverage
- Personal defense counsel retained to protect the defendant physician's assets
  —He or she will be interested in settling within the policy limits
- Dollar amount needed to reach a settlement agreement
- Jurisdiction in which the case will be tried
  —Previous jury verdicts in similar cases
  —Length of time needed to litigate the case to a conclusion
- Personality factors
  —Attitude of the defendant physician, who may be adamant to go to trial or may not want to invest further time and energy in the case
  —Adversarial attitude or position of codefendants
  —Strengths or weaknesses of individual witnesses
  —Skill and reputation of the respective attorneys
  —Judge's reputation

The possibility of a settlement may be discussed at any time. A case may be settled at the incident stage. This process often is referred to as aggressive incident management. The mechanics of this type of settlement differ from the mechanics of settlement of a formal claim.

Settlement of an Incident

- The physician plays a primary role, ensuring that:
  —The insurance carrier is notified.
  —The hospital risk manager or incident manager is also notified if the incident occurred in the hospital.
- Settlement depends on the response of the insurance carrier or the hospital
  —Further treatment of the patient at no cost may be suggested in exchange for release.
  —Some compensation to the patient may be suggested.

Settlement of a Formal Claim

- Attorneys play a primary role.

  —The plaintiff's attorney typically expresses to the defense attorney a monetary demand for settlement.

  —The defense attorney responds with denial, acceptance, or a counteroffer.

  —If a counteroffer is made, negotiations may continue, until the parties arrive at an acceptable settlement figure.

  —Demands or counteroffers can be made at any time, even if settlement negotiations have previously broken down.

- The insurance carrier plays a critical role.

  —Authority is retained to negotiate all settlements.

  —The defense attorney may accept a settlement demand or make a counteroffer only with the consent of the insurance carrier.

- The defendant physician's role depends on the rights contained in the policy.

  —You may not have the right to accept or reject settlement. The insurance carrier and the defense attorney can agree to settle without your consent, but you may be consulted about your feelings on the matter.

  —You may have the right to accept or reject settlement. Defendants with that right will be consulted before any offers or counteroffers of settlement are made. You will be asked to sign a written consent to a proposed settlement.

You should review the terms of your insurance policy to determine whether you have the right to accept or reject a settlement. In either case, you should be informed by your attorney of all settlement demands and counteroffers. You should be informed of the choices, the risks with each approach, and the alternatives that are available. Failure to keep you fully advised of settlement negotiations may constitute bad faith on the part of your insurance carrier if the amount of a trial verdict exceeds your coverage.

This is an area in which your personal defense attorney can play a significant role. He or she will serve as an intermediary to your insurance carrier and assigned defense counsel on settlement discussions and negotiations, will ensure that your rights are protected, and will pursue your remedies for a breach of those rights.

Take advantage of the expertise of your attorneys regarding the settlement. At the very least, you should be given an estimate of your chances of success at trial. To go to trial on an indefensible case that could have been settled would be a waste of time and effort. On the other hand, to settle a defensible case may set a bad precedent and may have adverse implications for your future practice and insurability. Try to be realistic and as objective as possible. Regardless of your decision, do not hesitate to make your feelings known.

Discovery Procedures

Discovery refers to pretrial procedures used by the parties to the lawsuit to gather and learn of evidence in order to develop their respective cases and to minimize the element of surprise at the time of the trial. These typically include Requests for Documents, Interrogatories, and Depositions but can also include Requests for Admission of Facts and Requests for Admission of Genuineness of Documents.

Discovery also can eliminate unnecessary issues and enable the parties to either settle the case or present it for trial in an efficient manner. Through discovery procedures, attorneys can assess the strengths and weaknesses of both sides. Because depositions are the most important of the discovery procedures for a defendant physician, they will be discussed in a separate section.

Interrogatories

Interrogatories are a set of written questions submitted by one party to the lawsuit to an opposing party, who must answer in writing under oath within a certain period of time. They can be more significant than most people think. They are admissible at trial, under certain circumstances, and can be used to cross-examine you at trial. For these reasons your responses must be precise, thorough, and truthful. It is essential that you and your attorney work together in drafting answers. Carefully review with your attorney all of the answers before they are signed and sworn to by you, and offer to assist your attorney in preparing interrogatories to be submitted to an opposing party.

Request for Admission of Facts

A Request for Admission of Facts is a series of factual statements, usually limited in number, served by one party to a lawsuit on another. The party served with the request is required to admit or deny the factual statements, in writing and under oath, within a prescribed period of time. Once a fact is admitted by the opposing party, that fact is no longer in controversy and can be stipulated at trial.

Request for Admission of Genuineness of Documents

A Request for Admission of Genuineness of Documents is a request from one party to a lawsuit to another. This request asks the opposing party to admit the authenticity of certain documents. In a medical malpractice lawsuit, the documents usually admitted by this procedure are the medical records.

Depositions

Depositions are the most important discovery procedure. Every party to the lawsuit can question the other party or any person who might be a witness. This examination, officially recorded and taken under oath, is admissible at trial under certain circumstances. Your testimony at your deposition has great significance; do not be fooled if it is taken in an informal setting or atmosphere. You should be just as prepared for your deposition as you would be for your trial testimony. The importance of a deposition cannot be overemphasized; remember that it might be introduced as evidence during the trial.

What Is a Deposition?

A deposition is a question-and-answer session in which the attorneys of both parties are present and involved in the examination and cross-examination of the witness. Its purposes are to:

- Discover facts and supplement testimony and evidence obtained from other sources

- Obtain admissions from the opposing party

- Lock in the testimony of a witness

- Learn the identity of other possible witnesses

- Learn the opposing expert's opinions and theories

- Narrow the facts and issues

- Evaluate the case for settlement

What Is the Procedure at a Deposition?

A deposition is taken in the following manner:

- The plaintiff's attorney begins the questioning and will be allowed to cross-examine you.

- The defense attorney will be allowed to object, when appropriate, and instruct you whether to answer the question.

- Your attorney may or may not question you.

How Do You Prepare for Your Deposition?

Preparation for your deposition is vital. Your testimony can be used to impeach your credibility if you offer contradictory testimony at trial. You should remember that what you say during your deposition is under oath. If you are not prepared, you might be trapped into saying something that you would later regret.

Prior to your deposition, you and your defense attorney should thoroughly discuss your knowledge of the facts of the case and the subjects on which you might be examined. It is very important that you and your attorney devote sufficient time to this preparation.

Review thoroughly the entire history of the case:

- Know your treatment and all pertinent medical records, X-rays, test results, and data.

- Review your own chronologic summary of the incident.

- Review the literature and any area of your specialty that may be the subject of questioning.
- Understand the alternative treatment options and be prepared to explain your choice.

Insist on a timely predeposition conference with your attorney:

- Don't wait until the last minute.
- Your attorney should question you and critique your answers.
- Your attorney should provide guidelines about testifying and review the danger areas and weak points.

Prepare for the opposing counsel's tactics with your attorney:

- Beware of questions about your mode of management that attempt to discredit your medical expertise.
- Beware of repetitious questions.
  —The attorney may ask the same question over and over again, with slight changes in the wording, in an effort to make you angry, cause you to lose your temper, or make a damaging admission.
- Beware of leading questions.
  —The attorney may be trying to get a "yes" or "no" response from you by beginning a question with "wouldn't you agree, Doctor…" or "is it not true…."
  —Do not let the attorney put words in your mouth. Instead think for yourself and restate your answer in your own words.
- Beware of hypothetical questions.
  —The attorney may ask you to "assume" certain facts and express an opinion based on those facts. Make sure that the "assumed" facts are consistent with this case and your opinion is consistent with your defense.
- Beware of definitions of "absolute standard of care."
  —Medicine is an art, not an exact science; there are no absolutes.
- Beware of concessions to authorities.
  —Do not always agree with everything written by one author or found in any one particular text.
  —Ask the plaintiff's attorney to specify the particular section of the text or article, review its language, and carefully consider your position.

How Should You Conduct Yourself at Your Deposition?

You must take the deposition seriously even if it is conducted in an informal atmosphere. If you have a strong case and perform well at the deposition, you might convince the plaintiff's side that it has no case. Most commentators indicate that the strength of the defendant's testimony is the most critical factor in a case. Even if you do not present well and you proceed to trial, the deposition is a good way for you to prepare for what is ahead.

Do not be surprised if the plaintiff is present at your deposition. The plaintiff and defendant each have an absolute right to attend all depositions in person. Your demeanor during the deposition will affect the outcome of the lawsuit.

- Learn to be an effective witness:
  —Listen carefully to the questions, weigh your responses, and think carefully before answering.
  —Take a short pause before answering a question; this gives your attorney a chance to object to the question if necessary.
  —Do not equivocate.
  —If you do not understand a question, ask for it to be repeated and clarified before you respond.
  —Do not be patronizing.
- Speak clearly.
- Do not ramble or volunteer information outside the scope of the question.
- Remain emotionally cool:
  —Do not argue with opposing counsel.
  —Do not show exasperation, anger, impatience, boredom, or fatigue. An emotional outburst may be used to discredit you at trial.
  —Do not allow yourself to be confused or appear to be confused by the proceedings; it may suggest that you were equally confused in treating the patient.
- If you do not know an answer, say, "I don't know."
- If your attorney objects to a question, do not answer it until you are instructed to do so.
- Do not go off on a tangent defending yourself. Your defense attorney may give you an opportunity to defend yourself with his or her questioning.
- Be honest, and do not hide facts.
- Do not be upset if the attorneys are friends and converse casually or banter with each other.
- Dress neatly, not ostentatiously; be courteous; take care in your manner, appearance, and remarks.

How Should You Conduct Yourself at the Deposition of Another?

Because you are a party to the lawsuit, you have an absolute right to attend all of the depositions in person. Unfortunately, this right is frequently disregarded, especially in view of the time constraints of a busy medical practice. It is extremely important to make every effort to be present at the deposition of another party. Your presence could have an effect on the testimony given; witnesses are more likely to tell the truth in your presence.

You should remember that testimony at a deposition is subject to all the responsibilities and penalties of testifying in court. In addition, attendance at the deposition of another party is informative and can aid you in preparing for your own deposition or trial testimony. You might also be able to provide on-the-spot assistance to your attorney in his or her examination of the witness. Although there might be a significant amount of time and expense involved (such as travel out of state for the testimony of the plaintiff's expert), it is often worth your while in the long run. Plaintiff's experts, in particular, might be reluctant to be critical of your care in your presence. You should ask your defense attorney about your attendance at these depositions. In some cases your insurance carrier might pay for your expenses to attend the deposition of the plaintiff's expert.

Trial

As your trial date approaches, you must clear your calendar. The trial should claim first priority on your time. In preparing for your trial, you should follow the steps you took in preparing for your deposition. It is vital that you become very familiar with the transcript of your deposition.

A large majority of medical professional liability cases are jury trials. Jury selection takes place immediately before the trial begins. Ask your defense attorney if he or she would like you to participate in this activity. You might make useful suggestions and can discuss your impressions with your counsel. This can be especially helpful if you practice in a small community and have personal knowledge of the people in the jury pool.

These cases often become high profile in the local media. You should refer media inquiries to your attorney. It would be in your best interest to discuss strategy for handling the public relations aspect of your trial in advance.

A typical jury trial consists of opening statements, presentation of evidence, witness testimony, closing arguments, instructions to the jury, verdict, and postverdict.

Opening Statements

In opening statements, the attorneys outline what they intend to prove or what the evidence will show:

- The plaintiff's attorney speaks first because the plaintiff has the burden of proof.

- Your attorney and the attorneys for your codefendants, if any, usually follow.

- A defense attorney might choose to reserve his or her opening statement until the beginning of the defendant's case.

- If your case is not a jury trial, the opening statements often will be shortened or eliminated.

Presentation of Evidence

The facts of the case are presented to the trier of fact—either a jury or a judge in a court trial—through various witnesses and exhibits:

- Plaintiff's case

  —The goal is to produce facts that will convince the trier of fact that you were negligent and that your negligence directly caused injury to the plaintiff.

  —The plaintiff has the burden of proving this by a preponderance of the evidence, which simply means more likely true than not true, or 51% likely.

  —If the plaintiff has alleged that you committed gross negligence, a higher burden of proof of clear and convincing evidence is imposed on that portion of the claim.

  —The plaintiff attempts to meet the burden by introducing evidence through witnesses, medical documents, exhibits, and the like

- Defendant's case

  —The goal is to prove either that there was no negligence what-soever or that the plaintiff's injuries were not the direct result of your negligence.

  —The defense attempts to meet this goal by introducing evidence through medical documents, witnesses, exhibits, and the like.

- Plaintiff's rebuttal

  —Rebuttal evidence is usually limited to new evidence that was introduced during the presentation of the defendant's case.

  —The plaintiff is given the right of rebuttal under our system of law because the burden of proof is on the plaintiff.

Witness Testimony

Witnesses are examined by both the plaintiff's and the defendant's attorneys:

- Direct examination

  —A witness is examined by the attorney who has called that witness to the stand.

  —The attorney may not ask leading questions, unless the witness is considered a "hostile witness."

  —If the trial judge determines that a witness is "hostile," in other words, that the witness might favor the opposing side to the litigation, the attorney who called the witness is permitted to treat the questioning as a cross-examination and can ask leading questions.

- Cross-examination

    —This is the subsequent examination by an opposing attorney of a witness who is already on the witness stand.

    —The attorney is allowed to ask leading questions.

Closing Arguments

In the closing arguments, the attorneys' final arguments to the jury are presented. In a court trial (with no jury), closing arguments are still presented to the trial judge, but they are usually shorter and more legalistic:

- The plaintiff's attorney speaks first, followed by the defense attorney, or attorneys if there are codefendants in the case.

- The plaintiff's attorney is given a final opportunity to make a rebuttal argument after the defense attorneys have finished.

Jury Instructions

The judge instructs the jurors on the following:

- The applicable law for the case.

- The legal principles and guidelines that govern the jury deliberations.

- Damages, which are not to be considered unless the jury finds in favor of the plaintiff on the issue of malpractice.

Verdict

The verdict is the formal decision or finding made by the jury or the judge:

- The verdict must be in favor of either the plaintiff or the defendant.

- In the case of multiple defendants, there can be a split verdict that finds in favor of some, but not all, defendants.

- Damages must be awarded to the plaintiff when the verdict is in favor of the plaintiff, even if the damages are a small amount, known as nominal damages.

How to Be an Effective Witness at Trial

Preparation is vital to your trial testimony. First review the "Depositions" section. All points made in that section are equally applicable to your trial testimony.

Your testimony at trial may be the single most important factor in determining whether you will win or lose your case. Your presence during the entire trial is useful, because it conveys your concern to the judge and jury. In addition to the facts of the case, a judge or jury is likely to take into consideration your appearance, professionalism, and manner.

Pretrial Preparation

Preparation for the trial includes the following:

- Review the transcript of your deposition testimony and the transcripts of the experts' depositions, especially if the depositions took place a long time ago, to understand the strengths and weaknesses of your case before the trial begins.

- Spend a substantial amount of time with your attorney preparing for trial.

    —Insist on a timely pretrial conference with your attorney.

    —Be sure your attorney is aware of the ACOG Expert Witness Affirmation.

- Have your family, friends, and even selected members of your staff present during the trial.

    —Their presence will give you moral support in this stressful time.

    —Their presence also will make an impression on the jury.

Trial Testimony

If you are going to testify on your own behalf, take the time to review how you conduct yourself on the stand:

- Always tell the truth. If two of your responses are inconsistent, do not collapse because your attorney can give you an opportunity to explain. There is no reason to panic if you are caught in an honest mistake.

- You must understand the question before you attempt to answer it. If necessary, ask the attorney to repeat or clarify the question.

- Be cautious in responding to leading or repetitive questions.

- Do not volunteer more information than the question calls for.

- Do not accept the opposing counsel's summary of your testimony unless it is accurate.

- Speak directly to the jury and do not talk down to them.

    —Make eye contact with the jury members and speak to them as frankly and openly as you would to a friend or neighbor.

- Do not look at your lawyer for help when you are on the stand.

    —The jury would notice this and get a bad impression.

- Do not be surprised if the judge asks you a question. You should answer it unless your attorney objects.

- Be articulate—speak clearly and audibly.

    —Be aware of your mannerisms of speech, such as mumbling or speaking rapidly and using "umms" and "you know's."

- Be respectful and courteous at all times.

    —Answer "Yes, sir/ma'am" and "No, sir/ma'am," and address the judge as "Your Honor."

    —Do not be smug or project an attitude of "I know it all."

- No matter how hard you are pressed, do not lose your temper.

    —Do not argue with the attorney on the other side. Remember, the plaintiff's attorney has the right to question you.

- Dress appropriately for trial. Flashy dress might convey that you are more interested in making money than in taking care of patients. Untidy appearance might indicate that you are disorganized and unreliable.

- Be aware of your body language because you might be sending the wrong message to the jury.

    —Also be aware of nonverbal communication or distracting habits. The potential for sending inaccurate signals to the jury is high.

- Watch out for hidden messages in body language.

    —Slouching might indicate a sloppy practice.

    —Placing your hand over your mouth when you speak could suggest that you have something to hide.

    —Folded arms might be considered a defensive gesture.

- Avoid these habits while on the witness stand: scowling, fidgeting, tugging at your ear, wringing your hands, and biting your fingernails.

- Rather than manifesting relief, triumph, or defeat when you leave the witness stand, you should walk with confidence at a normal pace.

Postverdict

A medical professional liability case does not necessarily end when a verdict is rendered.

- Your attorneys can do several things:

    —Ask the trial court to set aside the verdict and grant a new trial.

    —Ask the trial court to change the verdict by entering a judgment in your favor.

    —Ask the trial court to reduce the amount of the damage award; this process is known as *remittitur*.

    —Reopen settlement negotiations with the plaintiff, using the threat of appeal as leverage.

    —File an appeal.

- The plaintiff's attorneys can do the following:

    —Ask the trial court to set aside the verdict and grant a new trial.

—Ask the trial court to change the verdict by entering a judgment in favor of the plaintiff.

—Reopen settlement negotiations, using the threat of appeal as leverage.

—Ask the trial judge to increase the amount of damages awarded if the plaintiff won the case; this process is known as *additur*.

—File an appeal.

Appendix B

Qualifications for the Physician Expert Witness

1. The physician expert witness must have a current, valid, and unrestricted license to practice medicine in the state in which he or she practices.

2. The physician expert witness should be currently certified by a board recognized by the American Board of Medical Specialties, as well as be qualified by experience or demonstrated competence in the subject of the case.

3. The specialty, training, and experience of the physician expert witness should be appropriate to the subject matter in the case.

4. The physician expert witness should be familiar with the standard of care provided at the time of the alleged occurrence. In addition, the physician expert witness should have been actively involved in the clinical practice of the specialty or the subject matter of the case within five (5) years of the time the testimony or opinion is provided.

5. The physician expert witness should be able to demonstrate evidence of continuing medical education relevant to the specialty or the subject matter of the case.

6. The physician expert should be prepared to document the percentage of time that is involved in serving as an expert witness. In addition, the physician expert should be willing to disclose the amount of fees or compensation obtained for such activities and the total number of times the physician expert has testified for the plaintiff or defendant.

Approved by the Executive Board of the American College of Obstetricians and Gynecologists

Copyright © ACOG, July 2003

Appendix C

Expert Witness Affirmation

As a member of the medical profession and the American College of Obstetricians and Gynecologists, I affirm my duty, when giving evidence or testifying as an expert witness, to do so solely in accordance with the merits of the case. Furthermore, I declare that I will uphold the following professional principles in providing expert evidence or expert witness testimony.

1. I will always be truthful.

2. I will conduct a thorough, fair, and impartial review of the facts and the medical care provided, not excluding any relevant information.

3. I will provide evidence or testify only in matters in which I have relevant clinical experience and knowledge in the areas of medicine that are the subject of the proceeding.

4. I will evaluate the medical care provided in light of generally accepted standards, neither condemning performance that falls within generally accepted practice standards nor endorsing or condoning performance that falls below these standards.

5. I will evaluate the medical care provided in light of the generally accepted standards that prevailed at the time of the occurrence.

6. I will provide evidence or testimony that is complete, objective, scientifically based, and helpful to a just resolution of the proceeding.

7. I will make a clear distinction between a departure from accepted practice standards and an untoward outcome.

8. I will make every effort to determine whether there is a causal relationship between the alleged substandard practice and the medical outcome.

9. I will submit my testimony to peer review, if requested by a professional organization to which I belong.

10. I will not accept compensation that is contingent upon the outcome of litigation.

Name:

Signature:

American Board of Obstetrics and Gynecology Certification Date:

American Board of Obstetrics and Gynecology Recertification Date, if applicable:

Appendix D

Code of Professional Ethics of the American College of Obstetricians and Gynecologists

Obstetrician-gynecologists, as members of the medical profession, have ethical responsibilities not only to patients, but also to society, to other health professionals and to themselves. The following ethical foundations for professional activities in the field of obstetrics and gynecology are the supporting structures for the Code of Conduct. The Code implements many of these foundations in the form of rules of ethical conduct. Certain documents of the American College of Obstetricians and Gynecologists also provide additional ethical rules, including documents addressing the following issues: seeking and giving consultation, informed consent, sexual misconduct, patient testing, human immunodeficiency virus, relationships with industry, commercial enterprises in medical practice, and expert testimony. Noncompliance with the Code, including the above-referenced documents, may affect an individual's initial or continuing Fellowship in the American College of Obstetricians and Gynecologists. These documents may be revised or replaced periodically, and Fellows should be knowledgeable about current information.

Ethical Foundations

I. The patient–physician relationship: The welfare of the patient (*beneficence*) is central to all considerations in the patient–physician relationship. Included in this relationship is the obligation of physicians to respect the rights of patients, colleagues, and other health professionals. The respect for the right of individual patients to make their own choices about their health care (*autonomy*) is fundamental. The principle of justice requires strict avoidance of discrimination on the basis of race, color, religion, national origin, or any other basis that would constitute illegal discrimination (*justice*).

II. Physician conduct and practice: The obstetrician–gynecologist must deal honestly with patients and colleagues (*veracity*). This includes not misrepresenting himself or herself through any form of communication in an untruthful, misleading, or deceptive manner. Furthermore, maintenance of medical competence through study, application, and enhancement of medical knowledge and skills is an obligation of practicing physicians. Any behavior that diminishes a physician's capability to practice, such as substance abuse, must be immediately addressed and rehabilitative services instituted. The physician should modify his or her practice until the diminished capacity has been restored to an acceptable standard to avoid harm to patients (*nonmaleficence*). All physicians are obligated to respond to evidence of questionable conduct or unethical behavior by other physicians through appropriate procedures established by the relevant organization.

III. Avoiding conflicts of interest: Potential conflicts of interest are inherent in the practice of medicine. Physicians are expected to recognize such situations and deal with them through public disclosure. Conflicts of interest should be resolved in accordance with the best interest of the patient, respecting a woman's autonomy to make health care decisions. The physician should be an advocate for the patient through public disclosure of conflicts of interest raised by health payer policies or hospital policies.

IV. Professional relations: The obstetrician–gynecologist should respect and cooperate with other physicians, nurses, and health care professionals.

V. Societal responsibilities: The obstetrician–gynecologist has a continuing responsibility to society as a whole and should support and participate in activities that enhance the community. As a member of society, the obstetrician–gynecologist should respect the laws of that society. As professionals and members of medical societies, physicians are required to uphold the dignity and honor of the profession.

Code of Conduct

I. Patient–Physician Relationship

1. The patient–physician relationship is the central focus of all ethical concerns, and the welfare of the patient must form the basis of all medical judgments.

2. The obstetrician–gynecologist should serve as the patient's advocate and exercise all reasonable means to ensure that the most appropriate care is provided to the patient.

3. The patient–physician relationship has an ethical basis and is built on confidentiality, trust, and honesty. If no patient–physician relationship exists, a physician may refuse to provide care, except in emergencies. Once the patient–physician relationship exists, the obstetrician–gynecologist must adhere to all applicable legal or contractual constraints in dissolving the patient–physician relationship.

4. Sexual misconduct on the part of the obstetrician–gynecologist is an abuse of professional power and a violation of patient trust. Sexual contact or a romantic relationship between a physician and a current patient is always unethical.

5. The obstetrician–gynecologist has an obligation to obtain the informed consent of each patient. In obtaining informed consent for any course of medical or surgical treatment, the obstetrician–gynecologist must present to the patient, or to the person legally responsible for the patient, pertinent medical facts and recommendations consistent with good medical practice. Such information should be presented in reasonably understandable terms and include alternative modes of treatment and the objectives, risks, benefits, possible complications, and anticipated results of such treatment.

6. It is unethical to prescribe, provide, or seek compensation for therapies that are of no benefit to the patient.

7. The obstetrician–gynecologist must respect the rights and privacy of patients, colleagues, and others and safeguard patient information and confidences within the limits of the law. If during the process of providing information for consent it is known that results of a particular test or other information must be given to governmental authorities or other third parties, that must be explained to the patient.

8. The obstetrician–gynecologist must not discriminate against patients based on race, color, national origin, religion, or any other basis that would constitute illegal discrimination.

II. Physician Conduct and Practice

1. The obstetrician–gynecologist should recognize the boundaries of his or her particular competencies and expertise and must provide only those services and use only those techniques for which he or she is qualified by education, training, and experience.

2. The obstetrician–gynecologist should participate in continuing medical education activities to maintain current scientific and professional knowledge relevant to the medical services he or she renders. The obstetrician–gynecologist should provide medical care involving new therapies or techniques only after undertaking appropriate training and study.

3. In emerging areas of medical treatment where recognized medical guidelines do not exist, the obstetrician–gynecologist should exercise careful judgment and take appropriate precautions to protect patient welfare.

4. The obstetrician–gynecologist must not publicize or represent himself or herself in any untruthful, misleading, or deceptive manner to patients, colleagues, other health care professionals, or the public.

5. The obstetrician–gynecologist who has reason to believe that he or she is infected with the human immunodeficiency virus (HIV) or other serious infectious agents that might be communicated to patients should voluntarily be tested for the protection of his or her patients. In making decisions about patient-care activities, a physician infected with such an agent should adhere to the fundamental professional obligation to avoid harm to patients.

6. The obstetrician–gynecologist should not practice medicine while impaired by alcohol, drugs, or physical or mental disability. The obstetrician–gynecologist who experiences substance abuse problems or who is physically or emotionally impaired should seek appropriate assistance to address these problems and must limit his or her practice until the impairment no longer affects the quality of patient care.

III. *Conflicts of Interest*

1. Potential conflicts of interest are inherent in the practice of medicine. Conflicts of interest should be resolved in accordance with the best interest of the patient, respecting a woman's autonomy to make health care decisions. If there is an actual or potential conflict of interest that could be reasonably construed to affect significantly the patient's care, the physician must disclose the conflict to the patient. The physician should seek consultation with colleagues or an institutional ethics committee to determine whether there is an actual or potential conflict of interest and how to address it.

2. Commercial promotions of medical products and services may generate bias unrelated to product merit, creating or appearing to create inappropriate undue influence. The obstetrician–gynecologist should be aware of this potential conflict of interest and offer medical advice that is as accurate, balanced, complete, and devoid of bias as possible.

3. The obstetrician–gynecologist should prescribe drugs, devices, and other treatments solely on the basis of medical considerations and patient needs, regardless of any direct or indirect interests in or benefit from a pharmaceutical firm or other supplier.

4. When the obstetrician–gynecologist receives anything of substantial value, including royalties, from companies in the health care industry, such as a manufacturer of pharmaceuticals and medical devices, this fact should be disclosed to patients and colleagues when material.

5. Financial and administrative constraints may create disincentives to treatment otherwise recommended by the obstetrician–gynecologist. Any pertinent constraints should be disclosed to the patient.

IV. *Professional Relations*

1. The obstetrician–gynecologist's relationships with other physicians, nurses, and health care professionals should reflect fairness, honesty, and integrity, sharing a mutual respect and concern for the patient.

2. The obstetrician–gynecologist should consult, refer, or cooperate with other physicians, health care professionals, and institutions to the extent necessary to serve the best interests of their patients.

V. *Societal Responsibilities*

1. The obstetrician–gynecologist should support and participate in those health care programs, practices, and activities that contribute positively, in a meaningful and cost-effective way, to the welfare of individual patients, the health care system, or the public good.

2. The obstetrician–gynecologist should respect all laws, uphold the dignity and honor of the profession, and accept the profession's self-imposed discipline. The professional competence and conduct of obstetrician–gynecologists are best examined by professional associations, hospital peer-review committees, and state medical and licensing boards. These groups deserve the full participation and cooperation of the obstetrician–gynecologist.

3. The obstetrician–gynecologist should strive to address through the appropriate procedures the status of those physicians who demonstrate questionable competence, impairment, or unethical or illegal behavior. In addition, the obstetrician–gynecologist should cooperate with appropriate authorities to prevent the continuation of such behavior.

4. The obstetrician–gynecologist must not knowingly offer testimony that is false. The obstetrician–gynecologist must testify only on matters about which he or she has knowledge and experience. The obstetrician–gynecologist must not knowingly misrepresent his or her credentials.

5. The obstetrician–gynecologist testifying as an expert witness must have knowledge and experience about the range of the standard of care and the available scientific evidence for the condition in question during the relevant time and must respond accurately to questions about the range of the standard of care and the available scientific evidence.

6. Before offering testimony, the obstetrician–gynecologist must thoroughly review the medical facts of the case and all available relevant information.

7. The obstetrician–gynecologist serving as an expert witness must accept neither disproportionate compensation nor compensation that is contingent upon the outcome of the litigation.

Appendix E

Professional Liability and Risk Management Check-up

Informed Consent

Risk Management in the Office Setting

Working With Nonphysicians

Risk Management in the Hospital

Working With Other Physicians

Patient Communication

Medical Records and Documentation

Tracking (Reminder) Systems

Medical Professional Liability Insurance

Informed Consent

1. Do you make an affirmative effort to make sure a patient understands the risks, benefits, and alternatives to treatment before she consents to care?　　Yes ❏ No ❏

2. Do you set aside enough time to allow a patient to ask you questions as part of the informed consent process?　　Yes ❏ No ❏

3. Do you inform your patients of medically appropriate treatment options even if they are costly or not covered by insurance?　　Yes ❏ No ❏

4. Are you familiar with the general and specific laws in your state governing informed consent?　　Yes ❏ No ❏

5. Do you know if your state uses the reasonable physician standard or the patient viewpoint standard for informed consent?　　Yes ❏ No ❏

6. Do you provide notations or some other form of documentation to the patient's file detailing the informed consent discussion?　　Yes ❏ No ❏

7. Do you know the emergency circumstances that allow you to treat a patient without her prior consent?　　Yes ❏ No ❏

8. Are you familiar with the rules of your state pertaining to informed consent for minors?　　Yes ❏ No ❏

9. Do you have an office protocol to document a patient's informed refusal of a recommended treatment or procedure?　　Yes ❏ No ❏

10. Do you obtain informed consent when prescribing drugs or performing minor, office-based procedures?　　Yes ❏ No ❏

11. When obtaining informed consent for genetic screening tests, do you discuss the possible need for the patient to share the results with relatives who might be at risk?　　Yes ❏ No ❏

12. Are you familiar with the requirements in your state regarding written informed consent forms?　　Yes ❏ No ❏

13. Does your consent form incorporate a description of the test or procedure, its risks and expected outcomes, alternatives, and risks of no treatment?　　Yes ❏ No ❏

14. If a patient will be hospitalized, do you obtain her informed consent before she is admitted to the hospital?　　Yes ❏ No ❏

Risk Management in the Office Setting

1. Do you tell your staff not to overschedule appointments?   Yes ☐   No ☐

2. Upon arrival, are your patients given an estimated waiting time?   Yes ☐   No ☐

3. Is your reception area clean and comfortable?   Yes ☐   No ☐

4. Do you or a designated staff member obtain a complete patient history for new patients?   Yes ☐   No ☐

5. If a staff member obtains a new patient's history, do you review it?   Yes ☐   No ☐

6. Do you have a method for assessing and identifying high-risk pregnancies?   Yes ☐   No ☐

7. Do you and your staff document communications with a patient on her chart?   Yes ☐   No ☐

8. Are telephone and other conversations concerning patients held in a private location where they cannot be overheard by anybody else?   Yes ☐   No ☐

9. Do you have protocols for staff to follow in handling patient telephone calls?   Yes ☐   No ☐

10. Do you tell nonclinical staff not to provide medical advice over the telephone?   Yes ☐   No ☐

11. Is your office in compliance with all relevant federal, state, and local requirements?   Yes ☐   No ☐

12. Do you have all necessary emergency equipment for treating possible complications of procedures performed in the office?   Yes ☐   No ☐

13. Do you have a system for tracking laboratory and diagnostic test results, consultations and referrals, and return appointments?   Yes ☐   No ☐

Working With Nonphysicians

1. Have you authorized any nonphysician personnel to act on your behalf at work?   Yes ❑   No ❑

2. Do you supervise or direct the employees of another?   Yes ❑   No ❑

3. Have you delegated any duties to nonphysician personnel that require medically licensed professional judgment?   Yes ❑   No ❑

4. Do licensed nonphysician personnel (eg, nurses, certified nurse midwives, ultrasonographers) perform tasks outside the scope of their licenses?   Yes ❑   No ❑

5. Do you advise nonphysician personnel to direct any questions about orders to you for clarification?   Yes ❑   No ❑

6. Are there guidelines in place for office staff regarding telephone communications with patients?   Yes ❑   No ❑

7. Are your staff members aware of the extent of their responsibilities?   Yes ❑   No ❑

Risk Management in the Hospital

1. Do you discuss the details of your patient's hospitalization with her prior to her admission to the hospital?   Yes ❏   No ❏

2. Is the patient's record accurate and up-to-date when it is transferred to the hospital?   Yes ❏   No ❏

3. Are subsequent patient encounters, whether in the office or elsewhere, entered into the patient's prenatal record at the hospital?   Yes ❏   No ❏

4. If another physician is involved in the care of your patient, have you discussed the circumstances with your patient?   Yes ❏   No ❏

5. Do you use a standardized approach to patient "handoff" communications (ie, transfer of care), including an opportunity to ask and respond to questions?   Yes ❏   No ❏

6. Are you aware of your hospital's policies and protocols related to the treatment your patient will receive?   Yes ❏   No ❏

7. Have you had the appropriate training for any new technology you intend to use?   Yes ❏   No ❏

8. Do you notify your patient that residents or medical students may be involved in her care?   Yes ❏   No ❏

9. Do you keep residents up-to-date on the status of your patients for whom they provide care?   Yes ❏   No ❏

10. Do you review all resident notations in the medical record?   Yes ❏   No ❏

11. Do you conduct a "time out" before operative procedures to verify correct patient, procedure, site, and if applicable, implants?   Yes ❏   No ❏

12. Do you mark the operative site if it involves laterality?   Yes ❏   No ❏

Working With Other Physicians

1. Do you limit your notations in the patients' charts to facts and clinical judgments?   Yes ❑   No ❑

2. When you make arrangements to have your practice covered, do you communicate this to your patients and document the discussion?   Yes ❑   No ❑

3. Do you use commonly accepted medical terminology and abbreviations consistently in your patients' records?   Yes ❑   No ❑

4. Do you promptly refer a patient to another physician or seek consultation when necessary?   Yes ❑   No ❑

5. Do you clearly document your recommendations for referrals in the patients' charts?   Yes ❑   No ❑

6. Do you communicate with the infant's physician regarding pertinent maternal health issues?   Yes ❑   No ❑

Patient Communication

1. Do you routinely ask patients by which name they wish to be addressed?   Yes ❏   No ❏

2. Do you communicate with patients in clear nontechnical language?   Yes ❏   No ❏

3. Do you take into consideration each patient's level of health literacy?   Yes ❏   No ❏

4. Do you explain the use, dosage, expected benefits, and possible side effects of prescribed medication?   Yes ❏   No ❏

5. Do you provide patients with regular updates on their treatment and condition?   Yes ❏   No ❏

6. Are you familiar with your obligations to patients with communication disabilities under the Americans With Disabilities Act?   Yes ❏   No ❏

7. Are you aware of requirements under Title VI of the Civil Rights Act to provide language assistance to patients with limited English proficiency?   Yes ❏   No ❏

8. Has your practice developed policies for communicating with patients by e-mail?   Yes ❏   No ❏

Medical Records and Documentation

1. Are the abbreviations used in the patient's record generally and widely recognized?   Yes ☐   No ☐

2. Are residents aware of the accepted method of making entries in the medical record?   Yes ☐   No ☐

3. Is accurate terminology being used in the patient's record?   Yes ☐   No ☐

4. Are all members of the health care team dating and signing or initialing all entries in the record?   Yes ☐   No ☐

5. Does the attending physician review and evaluate all entries in the medical record?   Yes ☐   No ☐

6. Are all dictation transcripts reviewed for accuracy and signed before being placed in the record?   Yes ☐   No ☐

7. Does the medical record contain a comprehensive patient history?   Yes ☐   No ☐

8. Have informed consent and informed refusal discussions been documented in the record?   Yes ☐   No ☐

9. Are the notations in the record legible?   Yes ☐   No ☐

10. Are the patient's billing and financial records kept in a separate file from the patient's medical record?   Yes ☐   No ☐

11. Are record entries made in a timely manner?   Yes ☐   No ☐

12. Have any necessary corrections been made following the accepted procedure?   Yes ☐   No ☐

13. Are notes of all telephone calls kept with the medical record?   Yes ☐   No ☐

14. Are copies of all patient e-mails kept with the medical record?   Yes ☐   No ☐

Tracking (Reminder) Systems

1. Do you have a system or process for tracking laboratory and diagnostic test results, consultations, referrals, and return appointments?   Yes ❑   No ❑

2. Is the tracking system standardized, simple, and accessible?   Yes ❑   No ❑

3. Are multiple members of your staff expected to use the tracking system to prevent dependency on one person who may not be available at all times?   Yes ❑   No ❑

4. Do you follow your established policies and procedures when using the tracking system?   Yes ❑   No ❑

5. Do you enter the tests, consultations, referrals, or return appointments in the system when they are made?   Yes ❑   No ❑

6. Does the tracking system alert you when test results or other items are overdue or missing?   Yes ❑   No ❑

7. Does the tracking system prompt you to document results when they are received?   Yes ❑   No ❑

8. Does the tracking system prompt you to document follow-up with the patient?   Yes ❑   No ❑

9. Do you engage your patients as partners in the tracking process, eg, do they know the importance of completing the test or referral, how they will be notified of the results, and what to do if they have not received the results within a specified time frame?   Yes ❑   No ❑

Medical Professional Liability Insurance

1. Did you contact your state insurance department for information about the insurance carrier?   Yes ☐   No ☐

2. Is the prospective company licensed to write liability insurance in your particular state?   Yes ☐   No ☐

3. Have you investigated the insurer's financial condition?   Yes ☐   No ☐

4. Do you know whether the insurance entity is a Risk Retention Group or Self–Insurance Fund?   Yes ☐   No ☐

5. Is the insurer backed by the state guaranty fund?   Yes ☐   No ☐

6. Did you obtain a sample copy of the insurance policy and read it?   Yes ☐   No ☐

7. Do you know whether the policy is occurrence-based or claims-made?   Yes ☐   No ☐

8. Does the policy include tail coverage, if appropriate?   Yes ☐   No ☐

9. Does the insurer offer prior acts coverage, if appropriate?   Yes ☐   No ☐

10. Does the policy contain special provisions regarding per-claim deductibles or limitations on defense costs?   Yes ☐   No ☐

11. Do you know what activities are covered and not covered under the policy?   Yes ☐   No ☐

12. Did you have your personal attorney review the sample insurance policy?   Yes ☐   No ☐

13. Have you investigated the insurance company's underwriting criteria for termination, cancellation, and nonrenewal?   Yes ☐   No ☐

14. Do you understand the insurance company's requirements for notification of an actual or potential claim?   Yes ☐   No ☐

15. Do you know whether your insurance company has a right to settle your medical liability case without your consent?   Yes ☐   No ☐

16. Are you aware that all payments, including settlements, made on your behalf in a medical liability case are required to be reported to the National Practitioner Data Bank?   Yes ☐   No ☐

17. Will the hospital at which you practice accept the insurance?   Yes ☐   No ☐

18. If your insurance company or defense attorney has recommended a settlement, have you asked for an explanation justifying the settlement?   Yes ☐   No ☐

19. If you are being sued for more than the limits of your insurance policy, have you retained personal defense counsel to protect you from personal financial exposure?   Yes ❑   No ❑

20. If you have received a "reservation of rights" letter from your insurance company, have you retained your own personal defense attorney?   Yes ❑   No ❑

21. Have you kept your past and present insurance policies for your files?   Yes ❑   No ❑

Index